THE AUTOBIOGRAPHY OF A HEAD

by

ALUN BUFFRY

The Autobiography of a Head

by

Alun Buffry

Published by ABeFree Publishing, 2021

ISBN 978-1-8384401-0-7

Appreciation

Thanks to Mark Gibson for proof reading.

Thanks to ABeFree Publishing for formatting the paperback edition.
http://www.buffry.org.uk/abefreepublishing.html

Stanley Richard BUFFRY - (Jim) born 1913, Argoed, South Wales, UK; married Vera LANGLEY

Sidney Charles BUFFRY – born 1892, Cinderford, Gloucestershire, UK; married Margaret JONES born 1892

Richard BUFFREY – born 1850 Cinderford, Gloucestershire, UK; married Emma PARRY born 1853

Henry BUFFREY (2) - born 1814, Newland, Gloucestershire, UK; married Hannah COOPER born 1816

Henry BUFFRY (1) - born 1771, Newland, Gloucestershire, UK; married Mary STEVENS born 1786

Worgan BUFFREY – born 1737, Clearwell Gloucestershire, UK; married Margaret TYLER born 1745

Joseph BUFFREY – born 1716, Old Swinford, Worcestershire, UK: married Deborah WORGAN born 1711

William BUFFREY (3) - born 1670, Old Swinford, Worcestershire, UK: married Emme SMITH

John BUFFREY – born 1647, Old Swinford, Worcestershire, UK: married Alice REID, born 1667

William BUFFREY (2) – born about 1600 married Martha PERKES born 1804

William BUFFREY (1) – married Cecily HAWKHEAD

Margaret JONES – born 1892, Bedwellty, Wales, UK, married Sidney Charles BUFFRY

Richard JONES – born 1858, Bedwellty, Wales, UK, married Elizabeth born 1860

Vera LANGLEY – born 1911, Barry, South Glamorgan, UK married Stanley Richard BUFFRY

Alfred LANGLEY -, born 1881, Somerset, UK, married Bessie PALMER, born 1886

William LANGLEY – born 1850, Somerset UK, married Mary Ann SNELLY, born 1841

Joseph LANGLEY – born 1816, Somerset, UK, married Elizabeth WILLCOX, born 1816

Henry LANGLEY – born 1790, Somerset, UK

Bessie PALMER – born 1886, Somerset, UK, married Alfred LANGLEY, born 1881

John PALMER – born 1849, Somerset, UK, married Eliza BLACKMORE, born 1848

Robert PALMER – born 1816, Somerset, UK, married Hannah PURSEY, born 1817

JOHN PALMER – born 1786, Somerset, UK, married Lucy KING, born 1780

Matthias PALMER

ABOUT THE AUTHOR

Alun Buffry was born in South Wales in 1950 and lived there until 1968 when he moved to Norwich to study chemistry at the University of East Anglia. He graduated in 1971.

After leaving University, he travelled overland to India on what became known as The Hippy Trail, with little money or guidance and where he became ill. After he returned to Norwich, he became a follower of Prem Rawat, known in those days as Guru Maharaji and he remains a follower this day.

BY THE SAME AUTHOR

I will avoid saying that I was born at an early age because I cannot remember it. My mother used to say that I had been found under a Mulberry bush, so I believe her. That was February 1950, in Barry, South Wales.

In fact, I cannot remember the first three years at all!

Vera Langley and Stanley Buffry

I can put a date on my first memory, the 3rd of September 1953.

I distinctly remember waking up in a massive bed with my father. My mother was not there. We were about to go to pick her up from the 'Nursing Home' and to meet my new baby sister, Gwyneth.

We went in a big black taxi and I had to wait in the taxi with the driver whilst my Dad went inside the building.

He soon came back with my Mam who was holding Gwyneth. That was when I first realised where babies came from and that I was an exception. The nurses made them!

Gwyneth very kindly brought me a gift, a 'potato man' kt. All I had to do was get a potato from Mam and stick into it the arms and legs and eyes, nose, lips and hat and I had a potato man!

I loved Gwyneth from that point on, although now I have few memories of her during my younger years.

Gwyneth Buffry

Mam and Dad, in those first few years, ran a small sweet shop. I can remember standing there one day, the customer side of the high counter, looking up at the rows of sweet jars on the very high top shelves. Mam was like a giant too. I was not normally allowed in the shop, for obvious reasons.

Years later I learnt that during the Second World War, Mam had worked In a munitions factory, "putting round screws into square holes" as she used to say, lodging with a couple that I later knew as Auntie Alice and Uncle Bert, who were not actually related to us at all. In those days family friends were often called Uncle and Auntie for us kids.. Later in my childhood, we often went to visit them in Cheltenham. Uncle Bert taught me how to race snails.

Dad had been stationed in Cheltenham and served on the searchlights and as a chef. He told me that he and the other cooks used to have competitions to see who could remove the longest strip of peel from a potato without it breaking.

After the War ended, he took a room with Alice and Bert and also worked with them as a confectioner. That was where he met Mum, apparently. Dad's name was Staley Richard, but she called him Jim, for some reason that I never knew.

I have other memories of that time between the delivery of Gwyneth and my first day at school and three and a half years later. I can remember my cowboy outfit and gun, my red peddle car and my train set.

We lived in a large terraced house in Barry, not far from the docks, along with my Mum's parents, Nana and Grampy and also my mother's sisters, Auntie Nellie and Auntie Phyllis.. I can hardly remember Nellie as she died when I was a very young. Grampy had worked as a docker and liked a flutter on the horses. I can remember him feeding me pieces of fat from a pig's hock that he loved to eat; I hated the lean!

Bessie and Alf Langley

Grampy was the son of William Langley who had been a travelling showman and ran donkey rides on Barry Island beach, until one day a donkey kicked the then-young Grampy (Alf) on his leg where he had been kicked the day before in a football match; it lamed Alf for life and William gave up running the donkey rides after that. William was dead before my Mum had been born in 1911.

Nana had been a serving maid in a house before she married Alf. Her name was Bessie Ellen Louise Palmer. Years later, I learned that both families, the Langleys and the Palmers, had moved from Somerset to Barry to find work in about 1890. Strangely Alf had a sister called Bessie and Bessie had a brother called Alf, although not related. I discovered that decades later when I was researching family trees.

I remember most of my Uncles and Aunties on both Mum's and Dad's side of the family.

On Mum's side there was Uncle Bill and Auntie Lorna, who lived locally, with my cousin Pam. From Nelson in the Welsh valleys, there was Uncle Sid and Aunty Sal, who was really Sarah but called Sal by family and Stella by friends. Uncle Sid used to come line fishing with Dad and I from the Barry Island beach and pier (Barry Island was not at that time an island and was connected by road and rail and had a good fairground and popular beach. Sid and Sal had two children, Victor, who was a couple of years older than me and I used to wrestle with, and Ann, a couple of years younger than me and whom I had a huge crush on. Uncle Charlie and Aunty Doris lived in Winnersh, near Reading. They had two daughters, Anne and Audrey. Charlie was a photographer and showed me how to develop and print black and white films; he drove a motorbike and side car and took me to spot trains and take photographs of them as they sped past. I also remember Bessie's sister whom I knew as Auntie Sarah although she had been Christened Elizabeth Sarah, and he son Arthur, a builder, who married Hilda.

Auntie Phyllis was unmarried and lived with us.

Phyllis Langley

Uncle Charlie and Auntie Doris

Anne Orpin dressing me up

With Santa and Gwyneth

On dad's side I remember his own parents, Maggie and Sidney. They lived in Argoed near Blackwood, in the valleys. Sidney was a coal miner in the local pits. I remember being at their house when he came back from work, blackened with coal dust. Then, after he had washed, he reappeared, clean and white. For a while I thought I had two grandads, one black and one white. Sadly he died when I was still young, after falling off a ladder at work. He was a foreman and had asked somebody to climb a ladder, but the man had refused and, as apparently Granddad was not the sort of man to ask somebody to do something that he would not himself do, climbed the ladder and fell. I remember being told that Nanny and her youngest son, Maurice, along with her daughter Sheila, had seen Grandad standing at the top of the stairs and he had told them not to worry as everything would be OK. Then there was a knock on the door and a policeman telling them Sidney had fallen and died.

Sidney Charles Buffry   Uncle Maurice with Maggie Buffry

Apart from my Mum's Mum's sister Sarah, I never knew anything about the other siblings of my grandparents, although there were many and very little about my great grandparents most of whom were dead before my parents were born in 1911, (my Mum) and 1915 (my Dad).

Uncle Maurice was the youngest of my uncles, just about twenty years older than myself and unmarried. Sheila was married to Ken who was a prison warden. There was also Uncle Hayden and Auntie Delse who had two sons Gareth and Nigel, Uncle Frank and Auntie Rachel, and Auntie Margaret, and Uncle Islwyn and Auntie Iris who had two sons older than I, Brian and Idwell. Of course I met them all and remember them all, but we did not spend so long with them.

Mum and Dad had given up the shop after my sister was born and Dad worked on the railways..

10

My first day at school was the first time, I think, that I had been away from my close relatives. Nobody told me that Mam would be coming back for me, so I screamed so loud and so long that the school had to send somebody to bring back Mum!

School was OK. My teacher was Miss Vaughn. I was in a class B, usually in the top three in examinations, but they never put me up to class A because they said it was better for me to be in the top three in a B class than the bottom three in an A class. Mr Todd was our headmaster. I only got the cane once, on my hand, and it really hurt.

I was still about 5 or 6 years old when we went to London and had my photograph taken outside Buckenham Palace.

I remember going to Bristol Zoo, by train, one summer.

I was fascinated by the parrots, especially the one that knew my name, Gwyneth's name (she was still a baby) and even the name of the street where we lived. I ran back to tell my Mum and Dad. Mum said "Dad will think that's funny when he comes back!". It took me years to realise why he wasn't there. Years later, Mum told the story that whenever they lost me in the Zoo, they always found me back with the parrots trying to get that one to tell me my name and address again! I had a ride on an elephant too.

During the summer, trains filed with people from the Welsh Valleys used to descent on Barry Island beach, so we used to go early and then go home and go back at about 5 o'clock. What always amazed me was the amount of rubbish they'd left on the beach, yet the following morning it was clean again. The tide had come in and taken all the trash away. Years later, when I was eighteen and on summer break from University, I took a job with the local council department responsible for emptying the, bins and cleaning weeds away from drains. One of my other jobs, first thing in the morning, along with a gang of other regular workers, was picking up the rubbish from the beach.

So I survived junior school, got through my crush on a lovely tanned-looking urchin-type girl called Suzanne, survived my first kiss from the tallest girl in my class, Elizabeth and sat and failed my 11 Plus examination, I was given a place at grammar school after others refused theirs.

At eleven years old, I found myself going to a new school, Barry Grammar School for Boys, along with some of my friends and about to make new friends, but no girls. They had their own school. Instead of being a ten minute walk away, this one was a walk of forty-five minutes, up a hill, or else a bus ride. Of course my parents had to pay for the bus fares as well as the uniform and cap. My Dad was a labourer at the local train yards at the time, not earning a huge wage. They were giving me pocket money, school dinner money and bus fares. I made a deal with them that if I walked to school and back, I could keep the bus fares.

Now I had to study more subjects, some I liked and some I disliked. That included English Language, English Literature, History, Geography, Mathematics, Science, French, Woodwork, Latin, Welsh, Religious Education, Art, Sport and Woodwork. I hated History, just a string of dates. As for Latin and Welsh, why would I want to to learn languages that nobody spoke; very few people in Barry spoke Welsh and I had never met anyone that spoke Latin? Religious Education, or RE, also, was of little interest to me and was all about the Bible. To make matters worse, the same teacher, Mr Jones whom we called Tojo, took lessons in Welsh and RE. He was a boring teacher and very strict and mean. He once asked the class who believed in God. Those that said that they did not were given detention and a hundred lines. Stories were told that he had been captured by the Japanese during the war, although I cannot say that was true. My main interest was Science.

By the age of twelve I had been given a chemistry set and I loved it, mixing stuff together in the garden shed.

I remember well the first time I mixed sodium carbonate and citric acid together in water and it effervesced. I thought the two chemicals were eating each other so they were aware of each other; they were alive. That was an eye-opener for me, changed my religious beliefs and my world view; it opened my eyes.

The other teachers, all men, were a mixture of good, bad and simply bullies. We had nick-names for them all.

Apart from Mr Jones, the one I liked least was 'Biffo', Mr Bear, the Maths teacher, a small man but a real bully. He constantly hit boys or threw the blackboard duster across the room. At one time he hit me on the back of my head with a book. "You know what that's for Buffry?", he asked. "No, Sir". He hit me again and asked me again. Again I said no. He hit me a third time, harder, and asked me again. "Yes Sir", I said. I never did find out what it was for. Such a shame as Maths was one of my favourite subjects.

Mr Warren, "Bunny", of course, taught History, which I did not like. He was another duster-throwing bully. He also used to get boys to put their nose against the sliding blackboard and pull it down to try to hit their nose with the metal strip that separated the parts of the board.

Frank was the English teacher. He was one of the more pleasant ones.

Any boy could be sent to the headmaster whom we called 'Cel' (his first name was Les) for the cane on the hands. I only ever was sent once, by Biffo, but again I did not know what it was for.. God that hurt.

When I was about thirteen, everything changed again, as

the school became Barry Comprehensive School for Boys, admitting those that had not made it into Grammar School. It was more fair of course, but we found ourself invaded by boys that did not want to learn anything except sports, woodwork and fighting.

When we were fifteen we were allowed to choose what subjects we wanted to do for 'O Levels.'

I chose Chemistry, Physics, Maths, Biology and Geography. Because of numbers, I could not study Biology or Geography and instead I had to take classes in Woodwork and German. I was already having to learn French and was not at all interested in German. Everyone also had to study English language, English literature, History, Sports (Physical Education, or PE) and for some reason, Art. But I could drop Latin (which had actually helped with French), RE and Welsh

Sadly one of the Chemistry teachers, called Basil, was another bully and also a joker. He could not say that "Nitrogen Dioxide is a brown vapour" without laughing out loud and expecting everyone else to laugh too. He taught a lot of Organic Chemistry and quite put me off; a had another teacher for Inorganic Chemistry and physics.

As I said, it was an all boys school. The girls school was a mile or so away, so only the boys with bicycles could get there in time when we were all let out after lessons. The only other chance the rest of us had to meet a girl was on the bus. I didn't do very well.

Just about when I was fifteen, we were getting ready for GCE O Levels. Bunny Warren decided to tell each boy what he thought he would achieve. When he came to me, he said, "You've no chance. You've never passed a history exam in your life." Strangely that inspired me and I divided up the course so I could focus on just two thirds of it. The best questions came up for me and I achieved my second highest grade, after chemistry.

I played a lot of chess whilst at Comprehensive School and was quite good but it put me off when I realised there were so many books with set openings, responses and play. As my interest in the excitement of Chemistry grew, so did my interest in Astronomy and Cosmology and I became the organiser for the Astronomy Club and took on the responsibility of inviting guest speakers for after school meetings. I wrote to Patrick Moore. He did reply apologising as he could not come along to speak to us. Also I used to take star trails by keeping the camera shutter open on clear starry nights.

One day, after getting the film developed, I spotted a very strange looking saucer shaped object seemingly still on the photograph with the background of start trails. Was it a UFO? I took it to school to show the science teacher. He contacted the Home Office or some official and then asked me for the negative which he told me he sent in. Weeks later he said he had contacted them again but they said they never received either print or negative, which was strange of course since they had asked for the negative after seeing the print!

At the age of eighteen I took GCE 'A Levels' in Chemistry, Physics, Maths and one 'S" level in Chemistry, which I passed and was accepted for a BSC course in Chemistry at UEA (the University of East Anglia in Norwich). I chose that course because it was based on continuous assessment and not just exams.

To tell you the truth, although school was not that bad, I was glad it was over.. UEA was new phase in my life, of course, away from home, receiving a grant and being responsible for everything from paying my rent, my studies, my expanded social life, my meals and my drinking. Each student also had a personal tutor that served, supposedly, as 'in loco parentis' and was the person one was supposed to speak to about personal problems; mine was Dr Daynes, but not the sort of chap that one felt personal with – he as pretty well absorbed by chemistry. He did have a very beautiful wife though.

Barrie Dean, Nina and Myself

My first year was spent living in the student residences a few miles from UEA, in ex-army barracks on Fifers Lane. There was a free regular coach service between residences and the University Plain, where the teaching blocks were, the nearby 'Village', where the students union bar and concert venue was.

Jamie, Sarah, Nina, Nick, John Sullivan, Alun and Glenys.

An immediate advantage for me was meeting people from towns and cities across the British Isles. A huge variety of men and women from all sorts of backgrounds. I remember one guy used to say "Hi Man!". That seemed very modern to me. Nobody in Barry spoke like that.

During the first week or so, all the 'freshers' were invited to go along one evening to meet the vice-chancellor and drink free sherry. I never met the guy but drank a few sherries. It turned out to be a sherry drinking contest amongst some of the new undergraduates; two guys drank over twenty glasses each. One was taken to hospital; the other wanted to fight everyone.

The other advantages were that there were girls about, one could drink beer whenever one wanted (subject to opening hours) and there were bands to see.

At the Fifers Lane residence, where the coach dropped us off next to one of the girls residential blocks, there was a bar. Needless to say, that was the first place I headed to.

My main group of friends were Nick and Barrie, the lovely Freda, Angela, Marie and Nina. Later John Sullivan, Brian Smith, Jaime Mulvaney and Glenys and Rob White.

Nick Barnett

Going to rock and folk concerts was new to me. I had never seen a band live before. The first one was, Julie Driscoll and Brian Auger Trio, then Tyrannosaurus Rex. Over the following few years I also watched performances by Family, Fleetwood Mac, Caravan, Soft Machine, Fairport Convention, Joe Cocker, Free, Principle Edwards Magic Theatre, Curved Air, Hawkwind, The Third Ear Band, Al Stewart, Fred Wedlock and many others: I enjoyed them all.

There was a bit of a division between 'town and gown', as they said. I did not go into Norwich City very often in those days. Everything was available on campus.

I remember one evening, I was sitting in the students union debating chamber when some guy rushed in and said there was a group of 'skinheads' outside on the walkway beating up students. Everyone, including about fifty guys, rushed out and confronted them. The skinheads had baseball bats. I was shocked to see a couple of guys from chemistry run towards them and just grab the bats and start swinging. The skinheads ran away. I don't think they ever came back..

The academic year was divided into three, with two four week holidays at Christmas and Easter and about ten weeks during the summer recess. During those holidays, I went back to stay with my parents and family in Barry in Wales. I took a bag of dirty washing, which my dear Mum, bless her, cleaned. I was growing my hair long. They didn't like that, especially my Dad

That first summer recess, 1969, my dad told me he had found a job for me. It was with the local council, emptying bins, cleaning weeds from drains and cleaning the local beach, the one that as a child I had thought was cleaned each night by the tide. It was not easy work; I had to stand on the back of the truck and the other workers would chuck up the bins and I would empty them, placing sheets of cardboard along the sides so I could pile the trash higher whilst standing in it.

There were no plastic bin bags or wheely bins in those days. It was indeed a very dirty and smelly job. My wage, with double time for a Saturday morning, was £20 a week. On the beach in the mornings each team member collected something such as tokens from 'Crispy Crisps' or cigarettes. I was allowed to collect glass bottles which I could cash in and boost my wages. £20 a week was double my weekly grant! I was rich for six weeks. What I did not like was the blatant racism amongst my fellow workers.

I spent the last few weeks of summer 1969 hitch-hiking around England, visiting University pals in Guildford, Essex, London and Guernsey. I also went to the Isle of White festival where I camped over a few days and saw performances by Bob Dylan, Joe Cocker, The Who, The Bonzo Dog Band, The moody Blues, Family, The Third Ear Band and many others, often, though, from a distance as there were so many people in the audiences. I later read that over 150,000 people had been there, although some of the press reports did not read like the journalists had been to the same event at all.

So September came and I was back at UEA. This time I was sharing a room in 'digs' with my my friend Barrie from Taunton.

Barrie was actually the first fellow student I met, in fact in March 1968 when I had travelled to UEA for an interview. He introduced me to some of the music that he liked, such as Elmore James and played the guitar himself.

The room was let by Mrs Utting, a very stern looking middle-aged lady. The room cost us about £2 a week each, with breakfast, but as winter came it got very cold. We had to walk for about thirty minutes to the residences at Fifers Lane to get the coach to campus..

The alternative was to walk all the way to campus which took about ninety minutes as there was no convenient bus service and I could not afford a taxi and did not have a car. I did manage to swap the room for a space in a double room on campus with a guy who had a car. I was much happier there.

Several friends used to come round for coffee in the mornings after lectures, many of which I missed as they all started at 9 am, so I copied their notes.

UEA was a modern University. It was only a few years old by then, with blocks for studying Arts and Languages, Chemistry and Biology, two blocks of residences, Norfolk and Suffolk Terraces, a library and another lecture block.

During my second year, I joined the fell-walking club, the rock climbing club and the caving club.

 I wasn't so good at rock climbing but the three clubs all arranged cheap visits which I went on.

I walked up Snowdon, Ben Nevis, Helvellyn and Coniston and Scafell in the Lake District.

They were great trips that I remember well. I went into caves in Yorkshire and in Somerset where I had to do things like climbing underground waterfalls and squeezing through natural tunnels, one being called 'Bloody Tight', which it was.

We travelled in the Student Union van and stayed in climbers' huts. There was a great felling of comradeship and a sense of achievement.

I remember well the trip to Scotland. We stayed in a climbers hut In Glencoe.

It was all blokes except Ginnie, a delightful American student over here to study for a year. I did get the impression that some of the chaps would have preferred that she wasn't there but personally I think she leant an air of dignity amongst us.

My good friend from Barry came up from Southampton University to join us on that trip. Also my UEA friend Rob Cranthorne was there.

We climbed, or rather walked up, Ben Nevis.

On top of Ben Nevis.

We visited Keswick where Paul and I were refused entry into the pub because of our long hair,

The sign in the window of this Keswick pub read "We regret we do not serve gentlemen with Long Hair"

At one point in some sort of bizarre ritual, we all swapped hats. I was the only guy willing to wear Ginnie's hat.

Rob Cranthorne

Another good friend that I remember well was John Stott. He used to own a yellow van which he used to take extra people on walking trips. He was a great and sociable guy, another anarchist,

Students Rag week was also fun, towards the end of the third term in my second year. A group of us donned our white coats, called ourselves the 'Flying Doctears', EAR representing East Anglian Rag, and entered the Pram Race, just over twenty miles from Cromer, on the coast, to Norwich. Six of us, four guys and two gals, had to push a pram in turns, riding bicycles in between our turns to push.

Back row: Steve the pilot, Steve Allsopp, John Sullivan, Angela Le Page, Nina Boyd, Nick Barnet.
In front, myself praying and Barrie Dean.

We were the only team with a bloke as the baby in the pram. I was the first person to push, down the hill to turn right, getting faster and faster. I though, well this is easy. With great confidence I turned right and promptly the pram tipped over, our 'baby', John wearing a crash helmet and nappy and with his hairy chest, toppled out on to the road. The other guys rushed to make sure he was OK whilst the two girls rattled collecting tins. The crowd must have thought it was a stunt as the girls soon filled the tins. About an hour or so later, in the middle of nowhere in Norfolk, a wheel came off the pram.

Fortunately I had somehow been prepared for that as I had a spare wheel, so we changed it, as the teams behind us passed us by.

It was early evening by the time we got back to Norwich. We even went round the one-way road system.

Our finishing point was outside City Hall. I expected there to be crowds welcoming us. By then of course, the crowds had left. There was nobody there.

We phoned the Students Union and they said the van was out picking up stragglers, starting at the last ones, and had missed us whilst we were probably on the one-way system. We left our bicycles outside the police station and told the union to pick them up whilst we caught the bus back to campus and straight into the bar.

There were a couple of other stunts, such as 'climbing' the pavement in London Street, a pedestrian way, and being put in the stocks to have sponges of water thrown at us. It was fine until some student-hating idiot just threw the plastic bucket at me.

Freda 'climbing' the pavement of London Street, Norwich

One of my Chemistry friends, Steve, a local lad, was taking flying lessons and had to make up some hours, so he offered some of us a ride in a two-seater plane. I had never been in a plane before, but loved it. We flew from Norwich airport, which was much smaller in those days, over the City of Norwich and UEA, and out over the Norfolk Broads. It was not a long flight but seemed a lot longer. Thanks Steve!

That summer, 1970, I hitched around the UK again and went to another Isle of White festival that years starring Jimi Hendrix (just weeks before his death), Joan Baez, The Who, The Moody Blues, Joni Mitchell, The Doors, Jethro Tell, Emerson, Lake and Palmer, Supertramp, Donovan, Leonard Cohen, Miles Davis and others. There were 600,000 in attendance.

Those were the days. It was incredible to hear all those bands in one place over just a few days.

By my third year they had built another residential block, Waveney Terrace. Then a new students union building with bars and a concert hall.

By the time I started my third year, to tell the truth, I was getting fed up with Chemistry. Somehow, after I stopped believing in church and religion, I had thought that science would give me an answer to my questions on life and the universe. It now seemed to me as if science was just another religion, asking us to believe in things we could not see, like electrons, atoms and molecule; like gravity and the Big Bang. Also I did not like 'organic chemistry;, which did not seem systematic like 'inorganic chemistry'.

That year I took a room in a flat not far from the city

centre. That had good and bad consequences. Good that I found myself able to go to the city centre more often and even meet some locals. Bad because it distracted me from my studies.

Just before the Easter holidays in 1971, students at UEA held a sit in inside the Arts building. The cause was that an American student had been busted with Acid (LSD) and had been fined by the courts, but then he was to be punished again by being kicked off his course, which meant him having to return to the US and possibly face the draft and end up in Vietnam. I could see the injustice in punishing him twice, so I took my sleeping bag, some course work notes and books, a little camping stove and some tins of food and some hash, which by then I had been smoking with tobacco in joints for a year or so, and joined the sit in.

At that time I should have been studying in preparation for the exams a few moths later. That never happened, with all the music being played, people milling around, politics and smoking hash. It was great fun during the sit-in but it ended just before the Easter holidays when a meeting was held and it was decided to end it with a march up the road to the University offices in Earlham Park, with the possibility of continuing after the holidays. As it turned out, when the next term started, we learned that the American guy had quit and gone back to the US.

So I was in my last term heading for exams. I realised that I had far too much to learn in organic chemistry, about five think folders full of notes, compared with two of inorganic chemistry.

I had also turned against the idea of determining a students future in an exam; even though the course was supposed to take into account continued assessment, the final exam contributed to 80% and the rest of it just 20%, and half of that was through annual tests. I had spent a year on a practical chemistry project and a chemistry literature project which together amounted to only about 4% of the final marks.

I spent my last few days thinking I would not sit the exams out of principle and got drunk instead. I wrote to my parents telling them my views and intent and they quickly wrote back saying not to worry and just do my best.

So I did sit the exams. I had six exams, each starting at 9 am, six mornings in a row.

The first was organic chemistry. I was hung-over. I wrote non-stop for three hours, making a lot of it up, guessing some of it and of course there were also some questions I could answer. Inorganic and physical chemistry were next and I thought I'd done OK. The next two exam papers had questions on my specialist projects so I did well. I don't even remember what the last exam was on, maybe scientific German.

As it happened I graduated. My parents were unable to attend the graduation ceremony so I didn't go.

As a laugh and a gesture we printed our own graduation papers, calling them 'Bachelors of Hearts Degree' and saying "After completing three years of study at UEA, I hereby award myself the Degree of Bachelor of Hearts". We gave them out to the students as they left after getting their degrees presented to them inside St

Andrews Hall.

Then we went up to the University grounds and sat outside the marquee where the graduates were nibbling on sandwiches, strawberry and cream and drinking champagne. One of the more revolutionary of the lecturers, Colin Clarke, came out with a tray for us. There was a group of about six of us.

At UEA I also met a post graduate chemistry student or two. One was called Andy Monroe.

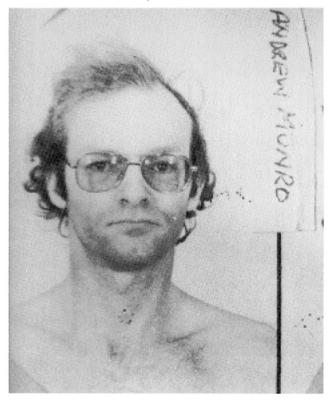

Andy told me that he was planning to make acid (LSD) and offered me a job when I returned from my travels. I never took that job. Several years later, the late 1970'2 I think, Andy became famous in the "Operation Julie" trials when a large group of chemists and others were busted for making and distributing millions of tabs of acid. Any was sent to prison for ten years.

Another drug he made was PCP.

PCP: Phencyclidine 2, 7, 11

I have changed the names of the people involved with this.

It was the summer of 1971. Zed and Ben had recently graduated in chemistry and were sharing a room in an apartment and trying to save money to travel. They were both 21 years of age.

After returning from a drinking session in the local pub, they shared a couple of joints and Ben produced a glass phial containing a clear liquid.

Zed asked what it was.

"PCP. Phencyclidine. They use it to make Angel Dust. It's a trip," said Ben.

Well, although Zed was quite drunk, he wasn't going to simply swallow an unknown liquid of unknown strength at midnight.

So he asked Ben where he got it and how many trips were in the phial.

"I don't know," said Ben, "I got if from Denny. She gave it to me to keep safe because her husband is in hospital. He made it. He's OK though, just took too much!"

"Wow, fuck, I'm not sure about that. Let's have a look," said Zed.

Ben handed the phial to Zed who opened and warily took a sniff.

"It's carbon tetrachloride," said Zed, "I'm not drinking that."

"I reckon it's dissolved in it 'cos PCP may not be soluble in water. So if we pour it onto hot water it may evaporate off and the trips will be in the water or maybe crystallize out."

"Yeah, OK, let's do it."

Denny was actually married to the chemist that had made the drug but she was also having a relationship with Ben. On occasion Zed simply went out for hours so that Ben could enjoy his time with her. Denny was not with them at that time though.

Having performed the experiment, they did indeed see crystals forming on the top of the water which they had put in a glass tumbler.

Ben suggested that they dip cigarette papers in to collect the crystals, as he said it was like LSD in blotting paper, but they did not have blotting paper. As Ben dipped a paper, Zed saw him lick his fingers. Another paper, another lick.

"Stop licking your fingers!" he said.

Soon Ben had placed six papers to dry out.

I think we should drink the rest," he said.

"Well I guess most of it must be on the papers," said

Zed.

"I'll get some orange juice and we'll drink half each."

Zed went to the kitchen and came back with a bottle of orange squash and a second glass. He poured half the solution from the one glass to the other, added some squash in and stirred it it with a pencil.

He picked up his half glass and swallowed half of it.

Ben picked up his own half glass and swallowed the lot. Then, without warning, he drained Zed's glass too.

Listening to some Jimi Hendrix on the stereo, Zed decided to write down his experiences on this substance and found himself a pen and notebook. Then he sat back, closed his eyes, listened to the music and floated away.

It wasn't long before Zen heard Ben moaning. He opened his eyes to see Ben laying on his back on the mattress on the floor, waving his arms around and frothing at the mouth. Needless to say, Zed panicked and started to wonder whether the same thing was about to happen to him.

So he grabbed his notebook and looked for his pen; the pen was nowhere to be seen. All there was handy was a yellow-inked pen. So he

picked up his yellow pen and wrote in his notebook.

"Ben is laying on the floor frothing at the mouth and waving his arms around, Foxy, Foxy Lady."

Hendrix was still playing on the stereo.

Zed wrote nothing about what they had consumed or

how much of it.

It wasn't long before Zed realised that Ben needed help but Zed was in no position to give it. It all became very real for him.

Zed by now was becoming very confused about what was actually happening and what was happening in his brain; he was becoming increasingly concerned that he may end up semi-conscious, like Ben. In fact, Ben looked unconscious now. Hendrix stopped singing and Zed put the record back to the beginning (it was vinyl in those days).

Zed decided to go upstairs and wake up Chris, whom he trusted.

As he started to climb the wooden stairs they changed into large stone steps, with plants and creepers down the wall, which was now like the face of a cliff. To his other side there was a long drop to the valley below. It was not so easy climbing the stone steps as they kept moving, but he made it to the top where there was a massive rough wooden door with magical symbols carved into it; stars, moons, pyramids. He banged loudly on the door, as one would do with a door that size.

Moments later the door opened and Zed saw Gandalf, or some other wizard, dressed in a dark blue gown with stars and moons on it. The wizard looked dishevelled and displeased. "What you banging for?" he asked.

It was at that point that Zed remembered he was actually upstairs in the apartment, talking to Chris, who was wearing his dressing gown and had just got out of bed.

Zed realised that in fact he had been banging on the bedroom door, rather loudly. There was no massive wooden door, no symbols carved on it, no creeping plants and no cliff.

He explained the problem with Ben, to Chris, but Chris seemed drunk and did not seem to fully understand what Zed was saying. Nevertheless, Chris followed Zed downstairs. As soon as he saw Ben, Chris suggested phoning a doctor. He told Zed to go out to the phone box and dial his doctor, whose number was 271127, while he, Chris, stayed with Ben.

Zed had no problem with that and the doctor, a woman, said she would be there as soon as she could.

By the time Zed got back home, the doctor was pulling up outside in her car. She went in to see Ben and straight away asked what he had eaten and drank; had he attempted suicide?

Zed was not keen on telling her that they had both taken PCP but wanted to tell her also that he was sure that Ben had not tried to kill himself. So he told her they had been drinking a lot of beer and that Ben had taken some sort of drug. She seemed happy with that but said she would have to call an ambulance. She left the apartment and returned a while later. It was not long before the ambulance turned up. They carried Ben to the ambulance and told Zed he could go along; they were taking Ben to a local hospital to pump out the contents of his stomach.

Zed was not keen on that, but agreed and went along. He noticed that the ambulance crew had numbers on their lapels. One was number 11 and the other was number 27.

Zed himself was experiencing both the outer world, which was looking very strange and magical, and the inner world which was filled with images and ideas. He felt as if he was thinking on several levels, and existing on several more. He remembered the number on the apartment was 7.

When they arrived at the hospital, they carried Ben on a stretcher to the inside to a ward and put him on a bed behind a screen. Zed was told to wait at the other end of this very large room. He could see a nurse and one of the ambulance drivers chatting down by the screened bed. They were laughing, probably flirting, he thought. Yet when he looked closer they appeared quite grotesque, their faces and bodies misshapen; they sounded as if cackling now, like witches at a cauldron.

Soon the nurse came over to Zed; she looked OK again now, and was smiling. She told Zed that Ben was to be stomach-pumped to remove the poisons. After that, she said, Zed could go with his friend when they took him to another hospital. She seemed very close to him, smiling and he could feel the warmth from her. Was she now flirting with him?

It seemed like a long wait, then the nurse came back and offered Zed a cup of tea, saying that in ten minutes or so they would take Ben to the other place. Zed refused the tea though; he did not feel safe drinking it.

It seemed a lot longer than ten minutes; in fact this whole episode so far seemed like several days but when they got outside it was still dark. Zed asked the time. It was three o'clock in the morning. They had only left the pub about four hours ago!

Soon they arrived at the other hospital and Zed followed as they wheeled Ben into a ward.

An extremely tall doctor approached Zed; he was quite lanky with long blond hair flowing behind his white coat, a stethoscope on his chest and a pair of spectacles that were much too big for him.

"Hi Man," said the doctor, "What's he on? It's a bum trip I think, but do you think he tried suicide?"

The doctor did not seem to realise that Zed was seeing everything multi-coloured and distorted, and his brain was operating at least ten times faster than normal. Zed was listening but analysing everything said on several levels.

Why was the doctor calling him "Man"? Was he a real doctor? Did doctors really talk about bum trips?

Zed did not want to tell that guy anything other than he was sure Ben had not tried suicide, that they had gone out drinking and then he had seen Ben take something but he did not know what it was.

The doctor character seemed to shrink in size and started to grin like a crazy man. A few more questions, not answered by Zed, and the white-coat guy who had somehow cut off most of his blond hair told him to go home and come back later.

So Zed left the hospital. Once outside he mused that he did not know where he was. He spotted two nurses and asked the time; it was now 7 o'clock. Time had passed very quickly since three o'clock. He asked what hospital it was. "West Norwich," one of the nurses answered.

"I have to get home to Earlham Road," he said, "Do you know if there is a bus going there?"

"Yes," replied the nurse. "Which part of Earlham Road?

"Near the Black Horse pub, said Zed.

"You can get a number 11 to the Castle," she explained, "then change and get number 27."

"OK, thanks," he nodded "Number 11 then 27!"

Zed had no problem getting home but he did in fact walk. It was just about 30 minutes walking and the sun was shining; he felt good although he felt bad about Ben and was worried in case his landlord found out or even the police.

He kept noticing that the numbers 2, 7, 11, 22 and 27 were everywhere and felt as if the Universe was trying to send him some sort of coded message.

He returned to the apartment, number 7. Chris was still asleep. Zed went to his own room, lay on the mattress and soon fell asleep. He awoke a while later and looked at his clock. It was 7 minutes past 11!

Zed still felt high; it was as if he had not been to sleep at all; but he had a strange memory of meeting Timothy Leary, the so-called "acid guru" and Jimi Hendrix. Leary had explained something about how the Universe was made of numbers and Hendrix had told him that music was numbers too.

Zed devised a plan; he would have breakfast and go back to the hospital to see Ben; after that he would go to see Ben's girlfriend lover, Denny, the wife of the chemist that had made the PCP and try to find out more about it. He hoped that he could leave the hospital with Ben.

So, Zed went back to the hospital. Again he walked and again he kept noticing the numbers, 2, 7, 11, 17, 22, 27. He asked himself what was the significance. Was it some sort of message? Was it a mathematical sequence? Was it some sort of reference to somewhere on a map, or maybe to a passage in a book such as The Bible? Of course, soon it became a game of simply spotting the numbers.

When he arrived at the hospital ward, he was greeted by a Matron who said that the doctor wanted to see him before he could see Ben, but that Ben was awake and recovering from his ordeal. She led Zed into a small side-room, where a doctor in his white-coat and stethoscope uniform sat behind a desk. Zed thought he was like some sort of witch doctor.

"Hi man," said the doctor, "sit down please. I'd like to ask you what your friend Ben took last night, because it was a bummer trip for him. It's better for him if we know what he took and why in case it was a suicide attempt."

"No, I'm pretty sure he didn't try to kill himself," said Zed, "He'd been drinking beer all night then I think he took a pill or something but I don't know what it was."

Zed did not like the questions. His mind was operating on multiple levels.

Soon the doctor said he wished he knew and then told

Zed to go out and along the corridor to room 7, at the end, where he could see Ben.

"Number 7? At the end?"

Ben was laying on his back alone in the small room, naked on a bed with bars at each side to stop him from falling out. As Zed approached, Ben looked up, looking startled.

"You are real! Wow I thought you were just part of my dream."

Ben explained that he had woken up and they said he was in hospital but the bed had bars on so he thought it weird and he may have been crazy. He said he had thought that Zed and the whole university time had been a dream. Then he said that he had been with Jimi Hendrix and Timothy Leary and they had given him some numbers: 2, 7 and 11.

Ben said that he had been instructed in the secret of eternal life. Somebody had told him that food was the cause of death and if we stopped eating and survived on only cosmic energy, we could live forever..

Zed was blown away for a while that Ben was talking about the same numbers and Hendrix and Leary although he didn't know about cosmic energy and not eating. He had eaten that day already, anyway.

Ben explained that he had woken up naked and didn't know where his clothes were. He said he wanted to see Denny. Zed promised to go to visit Denny at her house and tell her where Ben was.

On the way out he asked the Matron to give Ben his

clothes. She said that Ben was refusing to eat or drink so they were not releasing him, for his own good. He went back to Ben and told him. Ben was adamant that he was not eating or drinking anything.

Zen left and took a walk across the city, about an hour or so, and arrived at Denny's place, knocked the door and was let in by Denny herself. She was a slight but shapely lady with short fair hair and a good smile. She had a warm personality and Zed got on with her well, despite not really approving of her relationship with both Ben and her chemist husband as he was friends with both of them.

Zed explained what had happened and that Ben was OK but still in hospital, but when he told her which hospital she asked about the doctor. But Zed could only describe him, he did not know the doctor's name. Yet it did seem to be the same doctor, Denny said, as the one that had treated her husband. So she explained that she could not go to visit Ben. Zed would have to go back to the hospital to tell him. She made some tea and cheese sandwiches for Zed and then she rolled a couple of joints, which they shared.

Zen left and walked back to the hospital, He went straight into the ward and to the end of the corridor to room 7, quickly past any nurse, matron or doctors that could be lurking in wait. He walked into the room and saw a middle-aged lady sitting on a chair next to Ben who was sitting up in bed, now dressed.
He introduced himself as Ben's friend and the lady said she was Ben's mother, from London. The hospital had called her. She asked Zed what he had given Ben. She

was blaming Zed!

So it had become complicated now.

Ben's mother was blaming Zed.

The doctor said Ben could go after he had eaten and drank something.

Ben did not want to.

Ben's mother would only take him if he went back to London with her.

Ben would only go to London if Zed went along.

Denny and Ben would not be seeing each other for a while.

Chris was back at the apartment probably wondering what was happening; Ben and Zed would have to go there to pack some clothes.

Zed knew he was still under the effect of the PCP and he knew Ben was probably still tripping. He realised that it was going to be upon him to persuade Ben to eat and drink and get him out of there.

It surprised him when a few logical words to Ben later, having told him straight and simply that if he did not eat they were not going to let him go, Ben agreed to eat bread and some fruit and to drink water.

And so it was that the pair of them went to London and stayed a few days at Ben's parent's flat, way up in a high-rise block near Swiss Cottage.

The two lads agreed that they had both actually had a good time and the following day they felt normal.

Ben had arranged to have his eyes tested the next day.

They both went out, smoked a couple of joints and Ben went to the opticians. He later told Zed that the eye test was stupid and it was just lights moving around.

When Ben got the spectacles, he tried them once and then he threw them away.

Also during my last term several of us talked about and planned to buy a vehicle and cross the Sahara. I took a job with a local business building fences, living in several houses, then moving into a tiny flat with my friend John Sullivan, trying to save as much money as we could.

We didn't save much. John was one of the guys that I was planning the trip with. We discovered that crossing the Sahara was not going to be possible because we'd need expensive Carnet documents, so instead we set our destination on Turkey.

John Sullivan

One day, suddenly I had my first brush with the law. It wasn't for cannabis though.

Marie, Rob White and myself.

A friend, Rob White, was giving me a lift to visit some mutual friends who loved in a cottage at Keswick, just outside Norwich. Just a few miles from their cottage, I spotted what looked like pieces of firewood dumped on the roadside and thought that would do for their open fire. So we stopped. I had some hash in my hand, for some reason, and put it on the back seat of the car. We got out, Rob opened the boot of his car and I went to pick up some wood. Actually it was larger than it looked, so I picked up one piece that would fit in the boot. Just as I was putting it is, Rob said "Hey, Al, it's the police!".

I laughed but as I turned round I saw a police car, a 'Panda Car', as they called them in those days. The cop got out and walked up to us: "What you lads doing?"

"Well I am just taking some of this firewood dumped here," I said.

"Where you from?" he asked.

"We're students at UEA."

"Right, you are both under arrest for theft."

I thought he was joking. But no, he put handcuffs on us both and we had to sit in the back of his car whilst he drove us about five miles to Wymondham (pronounced Windum) police station.

All the police there were laughing about it. Then the sergeant came to our cell and said they did not want to charge us but 'Bill' (or whatever his name was, I forget) insists. So you are both charged with theft.

'Bill' drove us back to our car and told us to "fuck off now." The piece of hash was still on the back seat.

Several weeks later, I received a letter in the post, saying that I was being cautioned for "Theft of a piece of oak timber, the property of Mrs Margaret Unthank and valued at ten pence."

In fact that caution, like all cautions, is never spent and remains on ones criminal record for life. Years later, when I was in court, it came up. "1972, involved with theft."

The following day, after that incident with the firewood, still several months before our journey, John and I met Australian Paul, who became a great influence on us.

Australian Paul.

John and I had been walking into Norwich city centre.

We had been smoking some fine Lebanese hash the night before. It was a sort of green brown colour but when rolled between fingers it turned reddish and dark. A good sign.

As we walked close to Chapelfield Gardens, walking towards them was a large clean-cut chap with a smile on his face. Both John and I wore our hair long, which is probably why we were stopped.

The guy said "Hi, I'm Paul, just moved here from Australia. They call me Australian Paul, but back there they called me English Paul."

Paul had chatted a couple of minutes about who he was and then asked if John and I wanted to "score some dope."

We said no. Then Paul had reached over and dropped something into my coat pocket, saying "Smoke that later".

I realised it was a small lump of cannabis. I remember now how I had expected plain clothes "drugs squad" to appear and search and arrest me, but nothing like that had happened.

Instead, Australian Paul said "Tell you what Man, let's go have a smoke in the park."

So we, with me wondering what they were about to get involved with, went with Paul to the nearby Chapelfield Gardens where we sat, whilst Paul rolled a joint. We smoked it, then another.

I looked at the piece that Australian Paul had put into my pocket and it looked just like the Lebanese hash that we had smoked the previous evening.

Paul had said: "Tell you what Man, give me back that piece and we'll smoke it now. I live in Mill Hill Road, maybe you two can pop round this evening about 8 and we'll have a good smoke."

We smoked a third joint and Paul left, telling the lads the number of his house.

As it had happened, Paul lived in the very next street to where John and I were sharing that small flat whilst saving up for our trip. One could almost have seen Paul's place from theirs.

So at about 8 PM we gingerly knocked on the door, were invited in and met Lorraine, Paul's Australian wife.

Tea was made and then Paul produced a chillum. He warmed up some hash and rubbed it into some tobacco in his hand, poured it into the chillum and said "Give me a light man."

Paul held the chillum between his two clasped hands and inhaled through his hands.

"You know how to smoke this?" he asked.

Neither of us had ever smoked a chillum before, so Paul showed us how, first passing his clasped hands so each of us could suck on a hole he had made with his hands.

"Suck deep, man, from your guts, get a good hit."

Almost as soon as I sucked, I felt a rush to his head – the tobacco had increased the effects of the cannabis and I become stoned quite quickly.

Then John sucked on Paul's clasped hands.

Then we drank tea and chatted whilst Paul prepared another chillum.

This time Paul showed us exactly how he had clasped his hands around the stem of the chillum, so we could smoke it through our own hands.

It was not difficult.

Over what seemed like the next couple of hours we smoked several more chillums and drank more tea.

At one point Paul had asked me to make a pot of tea.

He place was a small bedsit and across the room from where we had been sitting, was a stove, sink and shelves.

I put the kettle on the stove but the tea caddy was empty. I spotted a packet of tea, put three spoons of it into the tea pot, poured the rest of the packet into the caddy and added the then boiling water to the pot.

Or at least, I thought that I had.

I had gone back and sat on the bed. I was looking across the room and I saw the lid of the tea pot seemingly rising from the pot! I thought I was hallucinating!

But when he had risen and gone over to the pot, I discovered I had actually put three spoons of tea into the caddy and emptied the rest into the pot! The tea had swollen up.

We all rolled around laughing.

After a while, I started feeling hungry and as we had been there at least three hours, I suggested to John that we leave and get some chips. John agreed.

So we left and walked down to the fish and chip shop that was not too far away, discussing the evening and how strange we had found Paul to be.

We reached the chip shop but it was closed. I had wondered what the time was.

The streets were very quiet for 11 PM but I spotted a man walking towards them and asked the time. Neither John nor I wore a watch.

"Quarter to three," said the stranger.

It had been quarter to three in the morning. We had been in Paul's place almost six hours!

With that realisation, both John and I started laughing. In fact we could not stop laughing.

We laughed so much, we ended up literally rolling round on the pavement clutching their sides!

But after a while the laughter subsided and we went home. That night I slept 'like a log'

In March 1972, five of us set out in a van, heading for Turkey.

The story for that trip is told in my book

ALL ABOUT MY HAT, THE HIPPY TRAIL 1972'.

To summarise that journey, I ended up travelling on from Turkey with very little money, through Syria, Iraq, Iran, Afghanistan, Pakistan and India, becoming sick and hospitalised with hepatitis and dysentery.

At the Iraqi border village

I managed to travel back overland as far as Tehran, where I became ill again, so flew back to the UK from there. That was an incredible experience that I would not change for anything, even though I could have died.

In fact, on my way back through Afghanistan, whilst in Kabul, I net a friend from Norwich who was on his own way to India. He gave me the devastating news that the evening after I had left John and my other friend Mike with the van in Antalya in Turkey, they had a crash and John had been killed, with Mike badly hurt and hospitalised himself in Turkey. That was several months since I had seen them.

I got back to Barry, in Wales, late September 1972, stayed in hospital there for a week, then stayed with my parents a few weeks recovering. My Dad said I looked like Gandhi.

Mum visited me every day, and one day she came again, with some letters from Norwich and a newspaper.

One letter was from two good friends, Pam and Steve,

saying that I could stay with them when I got back to Norwich and saying how sad they had been to hear that John was dead.

John had been a very much loved man and admired man by so many. Everyone that knew his was devastated at the news, they wrote.

But "stay away from Paul, he's taken up some sort of Guru called Maharaji", they wrote.

The second letter was from Paul, saying how he had given up drugs and was meditating on something called "Knowledge" that he had been shown by a boy just of fifteen years of age called Guru Maharaji.

There was another letter too, from John's parents, wishing me well and saying "John died amongst the people he loved so much."

I finished reading the letters and picked up the newspaper. I opened it randomly and there in front of me was an article about the "Boy wonder Guru Maharaji" that had come from Haridwar in India, an ashram called Prem Nagar, to bring his "Knowledge" to the West. There was a small picture with a caption that read "Lord of the Universe".

"How strange," I thought "that must be the place opposite where I nearly drowned in the Ganges. I wonder if that is some sort of child prodigy for that Maharishi Yogi guru guy that the Beatles had seen, but that was called Transcendental Meditation and now this is called Knowledge".

After a few weeks, I went back to Norwich, stayed with Pam and Steve, visited Paul and Lorraine and heard a lot about this Guru Maharaji and The Knowledge.

Paul and Lorraine told me much about their boy teacher, the Guru Maharaji, and the techniques that the boy gave to enable people to experience the "Knowledge" within inside themselves.

I was now actively seeking some sort of answer to an uncertain question about life and the universe. I started asking the 'I Ching',the book that Diane had given to me in Kabul, for guidance.

One day whilst I was about to consult the "I Ching" again, having thrown the coins and drawn the lines that would reveal the "hexagram" and reading, there was a knock on the door. It was Australian Paul and his wife and another follower of the Guru Maharaji called Alistair.

I did not want to be unsociable, so made tea, and then whilst the three guests chatted away, telling me once again about this "Knowledge", I could not resist picking up the book again.

The "lines" pointed me to read Hexagram 5:"The Waiting": as I wished that Paul would stop talking so that I could focus on the reading, I reached the lines that read:

"Six at the top means:

"One falls into the pit.

"Three uninvited guests arrive.

"Honour them, and in the end there will be good fortune."

It did not take me long to realise that the three uninvited guests may well have been sitting in my living room.

So I started listening and began to understand that Alistair, Paul and Lorraine were talking about some sort of experience within a person, an experience that he called peace.

Lorraine

Alastair Stevenson

I started going to public meetings about this Knowledge. The meetings were called "Satsang". I learnt that it was free for the asking but took commitment, "to yourself," the Guru said.

I decide to go to London and attend meetings and listen to the people that were then called Mahatmas, mostly men but also a few women and mostly from India. They were the people that initiated 'aspirants' into the experience and techniques of Knowledge. One simply had to ask for it.

That was not, for me, as easy as it sounded, as not only was a quite shy but I still did not believe it was genuine. I really wanted to find out if only to put Paul and Lorraine back on the right track. So I stayed in London, sleeping mostly on the floor of people that kindly volunteered to help aspirants. One day I issued some sort of challenge to 'God' Maharaji often spoke about

God that was the creator but that could also be found within inside oneself.

I shook my fist at the sky and said "OK God, if this is all real, then I want Knowledge on Christmas Day". That was just a few days away.

I went to a house in Muswell Hill, London, where a lady Mahatma called Prakesh Bai was speaking. I did not pluck up the courage to ask her for Knowledge, however. The next evening, I went back again and listened to her again. After she left the room a guy came in and said that anyone that had asked for Knowledge and told yes should put their name down. I wrote down my name.

On Christmas Eve there was a public meeting in a hall in Swiss Cottage area, in London so I went along. After the 'Satsang' speeches, one of the Mahatmas said he would read a list of fifteen people that would be able to receive Knowledge the following day, Christmas Day. By the fifteenth name there were only thirteen of them there, so he read out another two names, saying that if there was space the next day, these extra two could receive the instruction. I was number seventeen.

The whole of the audience started shouting to include us two, but the Mahatma said no, Guru Maharaji had said only fifteen at a time, but if we wanted to go along we could.

So the next morning I was up at about 5 am, walking from Earls Court where I was staying, to Muswell Hill. It was Christmas Day and God had heard my demand and I was to get Knowledge.

Of course the fifteen turned up so I was told to wait. I was quite angry. I left the house and hitched a lift back to Norwich. I was just down the main road from the house, put my thumb out and a car stopped.

"Where you going mate?"

"Norwich", I said.

"Oh good, that's where I'm going!"

So I had a lift all the way to Norwich.

As we pulled in to the Newmarket Road roundabout, just outside the city itself, I asked him to stop. I got out of the car and crossed the road and stuck my thumb out to try to get back to London.

The first car that stopped and he was driving all the way to earls Court. I was back in London before I knew it.

Three days later I received the Knowledge. I had a stinking cold, coughing and sneezing, but I had an experience that could not even start to explain. I knew then and there that this Knowledge was real. I still know that forty-nine years later, as I write these memories. It changed my life. I may even have saved my life. I have seen Guru Maharaji, now called by his birth name of Prem Rawat, many times since and always found inspirational and memorable. By the way, 'Prem' means love and his followers are called 'Premies'.

One day I picked up his "I Ching" again and asked "Who is Guru Maharaji?"

The result was the revelation of Hexagram 1 "The Creative" changing to Hexagram 50: "The Cauldron" with changing lines in positions first and fifth. You can read that for yourself!

That was a major changing point in my life. I had started reading scriptures, looking for an understanding but just became more and more confused.

When I was initiated into the experience and techniques of 'The Knowledge', just after Christmas 1972, I had amazing experiences that I cannot describe or explain. Strangely after that, I went back to some of those scriptures and they made sense.

It wasn't long before I moved into a communal flat (not a commune) where everyone living there was a Premie and followed Maharaji's instructions to do Satsang, Service and Meditation. Satsang, literally meaning 'Company of Truth' involved listening to others and, if one wished, talking to others, about The Knowledge.. Service meant doing for others without reward. Meditation meant giving oneself some time each day to practice each of the four techniques that had been shown to us, to focus on within ourselves, not on thoughts or mantas or anything we needed to crate, but on what was already there. I went to public Satsang meetings once a week in Norwich and spoke at them sometimes. They people that lived there included John and Kit, Australian Paul, Lorraine and their daughter Mara, Alistair, Peb and Trish and Neil McGuinness.

One day the most beautiful woman I'd ever seen walked in. She asked for me! Her name was Sue and she explained that she was the one-time girlfriend of Keith, who I had been to India with. Keith was in Nepal and had posted back some rice paper woodblock prints that he wanted me to sell and send him the money. I was far more interested in Sue that the prints but I agreed to what I could. I was instantly in love with Sue.

I had limited results selling the prints. I never had a relationship with Sue but we became loving friends until her sudden death in 2010.

With Sue Beswick outside The Great Pyramid, 1989

After a few months some other Premies opened up a larger house and I moved in there and took over organising the public events after Australian Paul, who had been doing it, stopped. That was probably one of the most blissful times of my life. I also took up a course in massage and acupuncture at a small private college called the Hua Chi Study Centre, run by Michel Quentin Hicks, although I gave it up after 6 months when he told us we should be doing it for money, not love.

I lived in that big house, in Westwick Street, Norwich,

for quite a few months, but I became aware that I had isolated myself from my friends and wanted to be able to tell them about Knowledge but they were not listening, so I decided to move.

I went to visit Paul and Lorraine and whilst there, a man called Paddy turned up and said he had a house to rent. I said I would rent it and the deal was done then and there. It was a four bedroomed house in Earlham Road, There were two couples at Paul's place that evening and they said they would rent rooms, I soon found more people and within a week I moved in.

Paddy turned out to become a very good friend and I spent many pleasant hours with him. Sadly he passed away in about 2012.

The house at 186 Earlham Road rapidly developed a reputation of a welcoming house. In the first few moths, none of my tenants were Premies. It was a house of alcohol and cannabis consumption, with lots of partying. That actually suited me fine. We definitely had some wild parties. One time, thanks to Australian Paul who was a constant visitor, over a hundred people turned up including a group of bikers who emptied one of the rooms, took up the carpet, turned up the stereo to maximum, and stomped the night away.

There was a lot of drinking and smoking of joints and chillums and almost everyone was tripping on free Acid. Half way through the night, the local drugs quad turned up, but soon left when they realised they were actually powerless.

Paddy Donnelly

I lived there for about a year, met lots of great people including Judi who I lived with for a couple of years afterwards, but then Paddy had to sell the house. I moved several times with Judi, through a few squats and then out into the Norfolk countryside to a small village called Holme Hale, which was a great place to live. Then to Wicklewood to a cottage called Windrush, near Wymondham (pronounced Windum).

Judith Dawson (Judi)

I shared the little semi-detached house with Judi and another friend, Annie. We had cats and chickens. The property was next to a farm.

One day a long-haired chap and his wife moved in next door.

He constantly complained about the cockerels crowing and the cats going into his garden.

1976 was a long hot summer. The sun shone almost every day from February through to September.

In about March, Judi and I had met some Argentinian guys in London.

One was called Poopee, and a poopee he turned out to be.

He invited Judi to go to Ibiza for a few weeks and she went. I was devastated at first. Three weeks later she was back. Poopee had 'dumped' her. That of course seriously effected our relationship, although we carried on sharing the bedroom if not the bed.

It was just a few weeks after that when I met a beautiful Argentinian girl called Basha, in Norwich. Her nationality was purely coincidental.

We had a very sexual relationship for many months. I found out she had another boy friend, also called Alan, a teacher at Norwich Art College.

I was surprised, to tell you the truth, but then again she did not seem like she could get enough sex. Not that I complained.

Towards the end of that summer, we were raided by the drugs squad.

I had about six cannabis plants growing in a plastic greenhouse along with some tomato plants and my long-haired neighbour had called the police.

I also had four ounces of Moroccan hash, which of course they found; also about a thousand pounds in cash and some scales. Judi and I were both arrested and charged with 'possession with intent to supply.

We were fined a thousand pounds and given twelve months sentences, suspended for two years.

Apparently the police had sat in the corn field and watched our house. One of them suffered sun stroke.

WICKLEWOOD

(written 2006)

They're watching us from cornfield there!
I heard the signs, saw smoke within the air.
Illusions? All in Buddha's many minds?
They watch, they know we're not their kind.

See there! The Wicklewood, road beyond,
Just secreted besides the Ducking pond!
A car, a scar, a landscape flaw?
Soon there's knocking on the door.

They came, they grinned, they even knew our names,

They played their endless searching games,

Seeking for a lump of hash.

Who'd have thought the law so crass?

Then by late 1976 I was living back in Norwich in a garden flat. Judi and I went separate ways after that, although we retained our friendship and I later became the Godfather of her daughter.

One day at that flat, there was a knock on the door. It was a chap called Donny Nice. He had a Welsh guy with him, called Howie and asked if he could leave him there for a smoke for an hour or so. I had a lot in common with Howie. We had both been born in Wales and been to University, we both had girlfriends called Judi and we both liked smoking good hash, which was Lebanese at that time. Years later I met him again, in 1997. It turned out that Donny Nice had sold him a passport in the name of Donald Nice. Donny pronounced his name as 'Niece'. Howie called himself "Mr Nice' as in he's a nice chap. Howie was **Howard Marks**, The Lebanese hash that we smoked, which was mine, had been part of a huge consignment he had smuggled into the UK! I became good friends with him after 1997.

I had a shock when my beloved Sue came into the flat one evening arm-in-arm with a man that I knew to be a bit of a scoundrel Wayne and announced that they had just got married. Wayne had been the boyfriend of Annie who had let Judi and I share her rented house in

Wicklewood, where we had been busted and Annie was about to come to France with Angie and I to pick grapes. That marriage did not last many years and almost cost Sue her house,

A few days later in September 1976, I went to France with Annie from Wicklewood and Angie who had been one of my tenants in Earlham Road. We hitched down from Paris to a small village in the south, not far from **Pont Du Gard,** a Roman aqueduct built in the first century AD.. In Paris, when we arrived on the road to hitch a lift south, there was already about two dozen people trying to get lifts. As is the etiquette, we walked to the end, the last people hitching. I put my thumb out and a car which had passed everyone else, stopped. He took us all the way south. In my broken French, I discovered that he was a chemist! So we talked chemistry a lot. We stayed at his house, met his wife and ate authentic home cooked vegetarian food. The following day he took us to Pont Du Gard, and left us. We happily slept by the side of the river under the stars for two nights. The aqueduct had three levels, one for cars, one for pedestrians, and the top, where we could also use to walk across the river. It was unspoilt by hotels and tourism in those days. Then the three of us easily hitched to **Dions,** the village where we were going to stay whilst picking grapes on 'the vendage'. Our host was Jacques Soulier - 'Mr Shoe'.

Mr Shoe's family had been picking grapes for years. Along with some of the other vendage families, they took on a few English as a status symbol. Because I was taller than the others, even though only five feet eight, I was given the job of porter, which meant extra wages and extra wine. I had to carry quite large bins of grapes, constantly being filled from the buckets used by the pickers, on my head, with just an old and part filled with straw sack. It was very heavy and I could not wear my glasses due to the sack. When it was full, I had to walk along a stony track and empty it into a tractor. As soon as I got back the tub was filled again. Eventually, the tractor was full and I thought I would get some rest. But no, they put up extended sides and a ladder! Now I had to climb the ladder with that on my head.

When we had started work, early morning, it was cool and damp. By 11 am it was scorching hot. We stopped for lunch that was provided, cheeses, bread, salad, cakes and red wine. We had a wonderful picnic in the shade, marred only by my aching neck. I decided I was not going to do that for two week, so I quit. Mr Shoe said OK, I could be a picker and he would do the porter job. He'd obviously been doing it for years. He ran with the bucket on his head. He said I would even keep my bonus wage and extra wine ration. The wine was only drinkable with meals, so we made sangria with fruit in large hollowed-out water melons.

I was a lot happier picking than portering.

The mother asked us to watch out of 'les escargots' (snails) which she cooked. I also saw Praying mantis, which I worried about as I thought they were deadly, until I was told they are only deadly to other insects.

We met some locals in Dions, of course, eventually learning of all their relationship problems. It seemed that nobody in the village had ever been on a plane.

Also while in the area, Annie, Angie and I visited

Nimes with its colosseum, Avignon with its famous bridge and beautiful cathedral, and the Camargue.

We hitched to **Aigues-Mortes**, a medieval walled city, and walked to the village of **Saintes-Maries-de-la-Mer**. The village became known as Notre-Dame-de-Ratis (Our Lady of the Boat in reference to stories that the three Marys had arrived by boat. That was Mary the mother of Jesus, Mary Magdalene, Mary Salome and Mary of Clopas (believed to have been the first three women to see the empty tomb after Christ's crucifixion, along with Sara, who some believed to be the daughter of Jesus. The name was later changed to Notre-Dame-de-la-Mer (Our Lady of the Sea, a synonym for the Virgin Mary). It is where the Rhone river meets the Mediterranean.

The **Carmargue** was famous for wild horses. To us it became famous for mosquitoes. Annie and Angie had to take a pee and their exposed bottoms became attractive to dozens of the pests and they were both bitten badly, also on arms and faces. I didn't get one bite. The three of us slept in fields under beautiful starry nights.

After that Annie went back to Norwich,

Angie and I decided to head for **Morocco**. She had been there the previous year. I had never been there. We found it easy getting to Barcelona but could not hitch south from there.

There was no good place to hitch and no cars stopped. So we took the train to **Cordoba**, visiting the famous and then to **Malaga**, from there by bus to **Algecires** and then by ferry to **Ceuta**.

Angie

Ceuta is actually a small part of Spain on the northern coast of Morocco.

From there one walks across the border to catch a bus to **Tetuan** and on to **Fez**. We stopped just overnight in Tetuan, which did not attract us. Fez was wonderful.

We passed some beautiful views of the Atlas mountains. The weather was lovely for late September..

Angie was good to travel with, easy going, plus she had her own money from the vendage. We stayed just inside the main gate in a hotel close to where the bus stopped.

It never takes long to meet a local in places like that. Our guide-to-be was called Mohammed Couscous.

Fez had two medinas and a more modern sector., the Ville Nouvelle. We were advised not to go deep into a medina alone.

Fez had been part of the French colonial section of Morocco, since 1912 until 1956. Mohammed Couscous did take us down into one of the medinas one day.

A woman started shouting at him and pointing at us. I asked us what she was saying. At first he would not say, then she said that she was shouting "Why are you walking with the dog people?"

Apart from that, we had found Fez a friendly place, with small cafes and elderly chaps smoking sibsi pipes of kif (cannabis mixed with black tobacco), which was legal for them, but not us.

A sibsi is a traditional Moroccan pipe with a long wooden tube and narrow clay bowl called a skuff. Yet Couscous was happy to get some good Moroccan hash for us. We stayed there about a week before catching a bus to **Marrakesh**. Again some superb views of the mountains.

MARRAKESH SUNRISE 1977

Many times we've sat,

And watched a good sunset,

But the beauty of the skies,

Of the Marrakesh. sunrise!

Behind the Atlas Mountains,

There's a desert full of fountains,

Lakes of pale blue ice,

And golden coloured spice

And yellow sparkling sand,

Suspended from God's hand.

Today a brand new life,

Completely free from strife.

Whilst it is true that most of the time in Marrakesh. we were indeed free from strife, there was one unpleasant experience. It was in the market square, which was full of stalls selling Moroccan goods along with story tellers, acrobats and snake charmers.

We were walking passed a stall selling leather goods. Inevitably we were invited to "look not buy". There was actually a really nice leather shoulder bag that I liked. I said I would buy it the following day as I did not have enough Dirhams and the banks were already closed for the day.

The dealer said he would change money but did not offer me a good rate so I refused. I said I would buy the bag the next morning. "Tomorrow no good," he said, "maybe world ends tonight." I said "if the world ends tonight then the money will be no good to you and the bag will be no good for me."

He became very angry, started shouting and waving a stick. Being with Angie, I took her hand a quickly left the inside of his stall. He shouted and pointed at us and people started looking at us as if we were thieves or infidels. We made a quick retreat back to our hotel, which was called the hotel Mus.

The following day I decided to go back and buy the bag, but as I approached the stall, alone this time, he came out again waving his stick and shouting at us. Needless to say, I retreated again and never bought that bag.

Apart from that, I enjoyed Marrakesh a lot. It did rain though.

Tea Shop Grass Top

Marrakesh in the rain

Slices up your brain.

Saw some opium tea pots

Smoking green grass tops

Sitting in tea shops,

Losing the damp strain.

After a few days there, we caught the bus to a small fishing village called **Mirhleft** that we had heard of. It was on the Atlantic Coast. A lovely place, we took a room which we shared with a French guy called Bernard, who spoke no English so I had a chance to practice my French. Right outside our room was a well which we often sat around. Trucks arrived in the street every few days and emptied water into a pipe that led to the well. We met a fisherman who said his name was 'Mohammed Pêcheur' that walked past every day and bought good hash and good fish from him.

We cooked our own meals on a charcoal burner in a traditional clay tagine pot.

Each morning, we simply had to put in some vegetables such as onions, carrots and beans, along with some fish which we ate despite normally being vegetarian, a spoon of oil and a spoon of water, a little salt and pepper, and left it on the stove.

By the end of the afternoon it was cooked perfectly and delicious just with bread.

Also around the well were other rooms. In one was a large friendly Moroccan guy that reminded me of Australian Paul. He sold hashish too and we spent time in his room smoking and telling each other stories. He had been to London and spoke good English. He had his son, about thirteen years old, staying with him. The boy spoke English, French, German and Italian as well as Moroccan Arabic.

One day as we left our room after breakfast, the boy was sitting by the well. He said he was making hash cakes in the sun.

He was mixing resin and whatever it was, into small black balls and placing them on a plate in the sun.

We used to walk just outside the village and wash our clothes in a water tank that filled with water coming through pipes from up in the hills; people used to also swim in it! Water from the tank was also fed to crops of vegetables in the valley leading to the ocean.

It was wonderful just sitting there looking at the scenery.

By the time we got back to the little hotel, the boy had cooked the little cakes. He gave us one each, which we ate.

A short while later, I was just sitting enjoying the high. I remember I was looking at my legs which seemed like mountains with creatures that were actually a few ants on the slopes.

Suddenly the mountain, my legs, just crumbled away.

I suddenly came back to this world as I saw Angie stand up, then fall over backwards and start shaking. I quickly went to her aid.

She was laying on her back. I said "You OK?" She opened her eyes and said "Yes, why?".

I told her she had fallen over and been shaking and was on the floor on her back. She just said "No, I'm not" and stood up. She was fine.

MIRHLEFT

Mirhleft is a village grand

Made of pink rock and yellow sand.

It's good to laze besides the sea,

And sit and watch, just you and me,

The sunset or the street outside,

Where nothing changes with the tide.

Mirhleft, village by the sea,

A place to stay if you'd be free.

A place to sit and rest a while,

Watch the donkeys single file,

Walking up and down the street-
Burdened in this sticky heat.
And I wonder why those men,
Walk up the street and back again;
Maybe it's to look at me,
Watching them whilst drinking tea?
Sitting outside in the sun,
Wondering what they do for fun.
Then I dream that we ride our bikes,
Or catch a bus or go hitch-hike,
Up the valleys, over mountains,
Rivers deep and magic fountains,
Fields of kif and grass and hash,
Where together we can rest, smashed!
But I return to hotel room,
Where all the morn and afternoon,
We can lay and smoke and play,
But in this place one has to pay:
Five Dirhams a gram:
"C'est n'est pas cher, man!"

We stayed in Mirhleft for about a week and then went to
Agadir. We didn't like it at all so two days later we
went back to Mirhleft for another two weeks. One thing
I must mention, the night skies. They were so clear and

wondrous, especially after a good smoke, of course. Stopping in Essaouira for a few days, we went back by bus to Marrakesh. and then on the Fez

Essaouira was a nice place. It is a port city on Morocco's Atlantic coast. Its medina (old town) is protected by 18th-century seafront ramparts called the Skala de la Kasbah, which were designed by European engineers. Old brass cannons line the walls, and there are ocean views. We met a young man there who supplied us with good hash at a good price

Back in **Marrakesh.**, it was starting to get cold and raining. We stayed not far from the market square in a small hotel called Hotel Mus.

After a few days, we left Marrakesh. by bus to fez, but an hour after boarding the bus, I had to get out and go back to Marrakesh. Angie had to go on alone with all the baggage. I hoped Mohammed Couscous would be at the bus station and help her, which he was.

GOD'S GAME

Left Marrakesh today, to Fez, but on the way,

Felt a lacking of some sort - forgotten my passport!

Got off the bus again, cursing my damned brain,

Went back to where we'd stayed. God's little game was played.

Amidst all this goddam fuss, in little Hotel 'Mus',

I got the passport back! But my head's about to crack!

It's started now to rain. I think I'll catch the train.

'Cos lover must be there and I wish I was with her!

Not possible this time, to use the railway line.

So I sit in sorrow, waiting for tomorrow,

When I hope that I can go, if rain don't turn to snow.

Well the money goes so quick, I'm gonna have a fit,

I want to smoke some stuff and call the Devil's bluff.

Illusions all around, and my head aches from the sound

Of rains and cars and mules and stupid tourist fools.

But writing down these lines has made me feel quite
fine.

It's just that I couldn't half do with along hot bath,

And get rid of the dirt, and wash my only shirt,

And jeans and socks and all, and go and have a ball,

In Fez.

Sure enough, having retrieved my passport which I had hidden under the mattress, the next day I took another bus to Fez.

Angie and Mohammed Couscous were both at the bus station to meet me. All was well. He had taken good care of her.

But then it got really chilly and damp. I was sweating in the bed, soaking the sheets, suffering headaches and pain in my joints. There was no way to dry the sheets.. I thought I'd get pneumonia. I said to Angie that we just had to get up early the following day and catch a bus to Tetuan, which we did.

As soon as we left Fez, I started to feel better, but still not well.

Then as soon as the bus arrived and we got out, we were approached by a street hassler, offering to show us to a cheap hotel. I said no and we started walking but he stayed with us. We found our own hotel, but he hung about and before I knew it he was in our room. I just did not have the strength to kick him out.

Then before I could say anything, he asked if we had any hashish. Angie said she had some kif (the leaf and black tobacco mixture that locals smoked) and showed him her little tin.

He grabbed it and said it was illegal and his job was to report us to the police, but, if we wanted he would just give us back and we could pay the "fine" to him. I said I was ill and we had little money. I showed him my wallet that actually had little money and he said that would do. Then he said he was sorry but she was stupid and that was how he made his money.

Then a strange thing happened, most unexpected.

I said it was OK for him, but now I was ill with no money.

He actually gave me half the money back!

We did not like Tetuan at all, especially after that. So the following day we took a bus back to Ceuta, boat to mainland Spain, and a bus all the way back to London, sleeping on the bus. That whole journey from Tetuan to London took us five days. We were back in the **Norwich** early December.

I moved back into the garden flat that I had left under the care of a brother, Jonnie, of a friend, Michael. Angie moved in for a while then we found another house to rent, in Waterloo Road.

It was 1977. I was 27 years old. I felt that I had done a lot, seen a lot, heard a lot and experienced a lot. I'd met some interesting people, been to some unusual places, faced and overcome risks and started to learn a lot. Yet there was so much more that I wanted to see, so many places that I wanted to visit. Egypt was high on my list, as was India

Yet between 1977 and 1981, I did not do a lot of travelling at all.

I lived in that house in Waterloo Road, with Angie and Ian Stevenson, the brother of Alistair whom I had met with Australian Paul and Lorraine back in 1973.

One morning, I woke up and felt that my vision was bleary. I ribbed my eye, the I smelled smoke. I jumped out of bed, stark naked, opened my bedroom door. Looking down the stairs, I saw only blackness.

Then whoosh, the hot black smoke hit me. I rushed into Ian's room. He wasn't there. I forgot to close my bedroom door and he window was open. That of course fed the flames.

The house was on fire. My first though of burning toast was way off.

I smashed Ian's window and shouted "Fire! Fire" at the top of my voice.

A nearby builder appeared outside in the back yard, with a ladder. I scrambled through the smashed window, cutting my side, and stepped over on to the bathroom flat roof, grabbing a sheet to keep at least some decency at the last minute. The ladder was now up against the roof, so I climbed down. I cut my bare feet on the broken glass from the window I'd smashed.

The back door was locked. I was still half asleep. I thought I could smash the glass on the back door and reach inside for the key which would have been on a hook near the door.

I grabbed the key. It was very hot and I immediately dropped it.

Within minutes I was inside the house next door which was occupied by English Moslems. It was not more than ten minutes before the fire brigade turned up and the fire was ousted. The guys in the house said they had been chanting upstairs in the bedroom when a vision of smoke started to appear rising through the floorboards. Then they had smelled the smoke and heard my shouts. Meanwhile the house 'Mother' who had been at the kitchen sink, said she heard a shout and looked through the window to see "a blackened naked hippy climbing out of the window, so I averted my eyes".

It wasn't long before I found myself standing in the gutted back room of our rented house, along with a fireman, a policeman and my landlord. Everything had been taken out of the room and dumped in the back yard. Even the wallpaper had burned off the wall. Strange indeed for the only thing left on the wall unburned was a small picture of my smiling teacher, Maharaji.

It made me feel how much I appreciated my life.

Ian suddenly reappeared. Unusual for him, he had

arisen early and gone shopping. Then, after I had told the cop that Angie worked in the library at the Art College, she turned up too. The fireman said they thought it had been an electrical fault.

The fire had just started burning the door to Angie's downstairs front bedroom which was next to the gutted living room. Most of her stuff was OK. Ian's room was untouched. Of course I lost my stereo, TV, some books and furniture from downstairs, plus all my books and clothing hanging upstairs suffered smoke damage.

The landlord said he had another house on the same road and that day, we moved there. That was another turning point in my life and major change in my philosophy and attitude..

We lived in that other house for a year or so, then the landlord said he had fixed the burned house so we could move back there. Also he wanted to modernise the house we were now living in. As it turned out the house next to the burned house, also owned by the same landlord, was empty so we moved in there. We stayed there a year or so and them moved back into the modernised house. At that stage, Angie decided to get her own place so I took over paying the rent and looked for a couple of suitable tenants. That was end of 1979, I think. It did not take long for me to find people to share with. Over the next few years, I had quite a few move in and out, some good friends and a few weirdo's. I was a lot more tolerant in those days.

In 1981, Judi, who was living in London, gave birth to girl called Melissa and I became her Godfather. Just months later, Judi came to Norwich with Melissa. She had left her husband who had a heroin addiction and needed somewhere to stay. My beloved Sue gave them a room to stay in until the local council in Norwich gave them their own flat.

Stanley Atkins

One of my tenants was Stanley, whom people called Fat Stanley, rather cruelly but also descriptive, as at five foot seven his waistline was 52 inches!

Stanley was what one called Old School, He was a bit of a scoundrel. His associates including some well known Norwich 'hard men', Joe Sharp and Levi McCarthy.

Levi was famous from running Mac;'s Cafe, out on the Yarmouth Road, a 24-hour cafe were many 'faces; went late at night. I never went there myself. During this time in the 80's though, he had calmed down somewhat and went into business with Kevin Franklin, a local entrepreneur. Using the front of the old cafe, they opened not one but three businesses and offered me the job running them.

My wage was just above dole money with the promise of more of they did well. First there was an agency, called Breckland Home Care, which was set up to find work for local skilled handymen such as plasterers, decorators, painters, roofers, almost anything, who would eventually pay us a commission.

To find work we printed fliers and hired people to put them through letterboxes.

To cut back on those costs, BHC, the second part of the business, would print and distribute fliers for other businesses and that led to selling, on commission again, fliers and other printed materials for local printers.

Then Kevin expanded the business to include EEC which sold communications equipment such as telephone answering machines and even TV projectors.

There were three problems with that. Firstly, when I answered the single phone, I did not know whether to Say Breckland Home Care, BHC or EEC.

Levi McCarthy

Levi and Kevin were like chalk and cheese, Kevin dressed in a suit and tie, Levi wore jeans and open neck shirts; Kevin wanted to give the impression that we were big business, Levi that we were just starting up; Kevin had all the brochures and information, Levi almost bullied people into buying.

The third problem is that we did not actually make much money.

As well as answering the phone, I had to deal with both customers and suppliers, I had to keep track on who owed us what in commission, organise the flier distribution, keep track of stock, do the accounts, write letters and even clean the office.

Well it did get me off the dole. I worked here for about five months, then my teachers Maharaji announced that he was going to speak in Rome again, so I booked tickets. Kevin and Levi did not want me to go. Kevin even offered me a bonus but I went anyway and when I got back to Norwich, I quit the job.

There was a story about Levi when he became a boxer for a while, at the Lad's Club in Norwich. For his first match, he turned up is a string vest with holes in and an old pair of shorts. He knocked his opponent out with one blow. So, apparently to teach him a lesson, they put him against the local champion. Once again, he knocked out his opponent with one punch. After that they said they wanted a showman, not a thug, so he had no more matches.

Joe Sharp had the reputation as being the hardest man in Norwich, not the sort of man one wanted to cross, especially after he'd had a drink or two.

Strangely they all seemed to have respect for me and never bullied me and that it turn gave me respect from a lot more people

We spent many hours playing the card game called Kalooki, a game like Rummy using 2 decks and 2 jokers, a total 106 cards. One had to make sets and runs and once they totalled 41 or more, they could be put face up on the table, if one wished. Then cards to be played on the sets and runs put out by the other players. It can be played with between 2 to 5 players. A complete game of Kalooki consists of several rounds of game-play, where players try to dispose of their cards as quickly as possible. Putting down all of your thirteen cards at once doubled the penalty the others players had to pay

I became quite good at it, often winning. We played for just a penny a point, often well into the night. The problem was that Joe did not like to lose, so sometimes I had to lose deliberately just so I could get to bed.

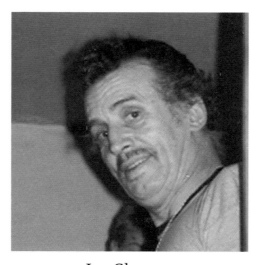

Joe Sharp

I played in the daytime too, with a growing number of people that used to pop in for an hour or so. I used to say "Don't play me, keep your pennies, you can't win", then take their pennies.

I did so well that even at a penny a point I earned enough to take my friend Hester to Greece for two weeks.

In March 1984, Hester and I caught a bus from London to **Athens.**

The bus took just over two days. We stopped for meals, but slept, or at least tried to sleep, on the bus. I took a small piece of hash hidden in a box of biscuits in a carrier bag of food.

At one point, in the then Yugoslavia, the bus screeched to a halt and the bag fell off the shelf with the contents including the biscuits scattered on the floor. As was well and I collected our stuff and put it back into the bag.

When we reached the border with Greece, the Greek customs wanted everyone to get their luggage outside and stand by it, whilst they walked around looking at it and sometimes into it. When they got to us, the guy just quickly looked into our carrier bag and walked away.

The journey down through Greece was through some very beautiful scenery. Fields full of red poppies and yellow gorse, mountains and sea. Some hours later we arrived in Athens.

Quickly we found a hotel called Artemission on Veranzerou. Wanting a smoke, I quickly found the packet of biscuits. It was open one end! There was no hash in it!

Of course we were both disappointed. I just took the other food out of the bag and lo and behold, there was my piece of hash just sitting in the bottom of the bag.

The following day, we went to see the Acropolis, down streets filled with shops selling brass ware, souvenirs, dresses and shirts and many kebab shops.

The Acropolis was built in the third century BC and dedicated to Athena and Poseidon. It was believed that the people there were the most favoured by the goddess and god. Athena gave them the olive tree and Poseidon gave them a salt water fountain, symbolising the sea.

Later the people moved down the hill and built the city of Athens.

Hester in Greece

So we spent a few days looking around Athens, seeing the acropolis and so on, then booked train tickets to **Patras,** in the Peloponnese.

The best part of that train journey was crossing the massive canal at **Corith.** Very impressive.

Patras was a great little palace on the coast. We found a great little hotel called Hotel Delphi, near the station.

Patras had a working flower clock.

I could not find good food. I had a tomato soup that tasted like tinned sardines.

Hester went for a walk and inevitably met a Greek guy that wanted to take her out. After that he kept hanging round outside our hotel and one day even followed us until I turned faced him and he just walked passed. He left her alone after that and she said that she'd learned not to go walking on her own.

We took a local bus to the beach, Plage Kourouta. Hester donned her bikini and despite the sun lotion became quite red quite quickly.

Whilst there we took a day trip by train to Diakofte, along the coast, to travel on a push-and-pull steam train to Kalavrita, weaving up to the mountain town of Kalavrita through hand-carved tunnels and plane-tree forests. Crossing 49 bridges as the Vouraikos River ran below. The driver was very helpful and pointed out the best views.

Patras was full of colourful posters and flags, with loudspeakers blasting out political propaganda before the elections, with a socialist on one side and a communist on the other. The Greek people seemed to take it quite seriously, always talking in loud voices.

Whenever we had to ask directions, at least three or four people got involved!

We spent a few days there in Patras, then took a train to Olympia, the site of the original Olympic games. We had to change trains at Pyrgos, The scenery was exceptionally lush.

Olympia was a very small town in those days with not many tourists. We stayed in the hotel Poseidon. Apparently the town had to be moved when they found the original games site beneath it.

Η παλαίστρα.   The Palaistra.

IO 371651

ΙΕΡΟ ΟΛΥΜΠΙΑΣ

ΕΙΣΙΤΗΡΙΟ
ΔΡΧ. **100**
DR.

I really enjoyed our short stay in Olympia.

We journey on by bus, passing though Tripoli and Sparti and arriving in **Mystra**, a small village at the foot of Mount Tougetes, also known as Mizithra. Here are the ruins of a Byzantine city. We stayed at Hotel Byzantine.

That was both beautiful and fascinating as we walked up the hillside passing buildings from various ages on the way, with fantastic views on the way.

After leaving Mystras, we headed for **Gythion**, a very small fishing village close to the undergrounds lake caves at **Diros** which we wanted to see.

We stayed at the Hotel Karanah.

We caught a local bus to Pirgos Dirou and Spilea Dirou.

Those caves certainly lived up to their reputation. Upon entering, we boarded a boat which took us through the caves which were well lit with fantastic formations of stalactites and stalagmites.

In Gythion itself, in a bar, we met an elderly Greek fisherman called Yannie. Through his broken English he told us in a hushed voice that he was a secret Royalist.

Holiday more or less over, we headed back to Athens, where after a few days, we faced the long coach ride, ferry and train back to Norwich. I would not say I was glad to be back. I had had a great two weeks with Hester.

On November 10th 1984, I left the UK again, this time with a girl called Helen, to visit **Crete**. We flew into

Helen Clarke

Athens and found a room in the Hotel Cleo, in Sintagma Square. We visited the acropolis of course, then had an evening meal of swordfish and salad.

The following day, after looking in some local shops, we went to the port, **Pineaus,** to take a boat to Iraklion in Crete, where we stayed in a hotel with the inspired name of Hotel Iraklion.

Iraklion itself did not seem to have much to offer, but we did visit Knossos where we saw ruins of Royal Palaces and a large area of ancient three and four storey buildings.

On November 15th we caught a bus to **Matala**. I had noticed the painting in Knossos but had not seen anyone looking like those people until, on this bus ride, I saw a woman with a child and they both had faces like on the ancient paintings.

Matala was small seaside place with beach and caves that people sometimes lived in.

Matala was a party place, just what Helen liked. But it wasn't for me so I left her there promising to meet her back on Iraklion a couple of weeks later, which I did, and took the hotel phone number so I could phone and give her the number of my hotel, across the bay in **Agia Galini.** It wasn't far away but I had to change bus twice, once at Phaestos, then again at Timboki, but that took only one hour.

I took a room with a balcony at the Hotel Akteon. This was quiet fishing village and I soon made friends, Gerry, a Canadian, who had a car, Alain, a French guy, and a guy with one arm fitted with a claw, from South Africa. He had his arm blown off by a grenade, he said. Joan Collins' daughter also lived there. She was very beautiful.

I was told that it was very safe there, no thieves unless they came from Athens. Nevertheless, I kept my door locked both when I went out and when I was inside.

One afternoon, I was resting on my bed and I heard a voice from Gerry's room next to mine, saying "Hello, how many people in this room?"

Then a scuffle sound and a cry of "Stop! Thief."

I quickly jumped off the bed and got to my door.

Outside on the balcony was the South African guy with his 'claw' firmly round the neck on a small chap who was struggling to get free.

"He's got my bag", shouted Gerry. The South African punched the other guy in the face; he dropped the bag, the grip was loosened and the guy ran off. Gerry left the next day.

I spent a few days visiting other places around the island, travelling by bus. As it was out of season, everywhere was quiet now.

I visited **Agia Nikolas,, Sitia, Vai** and **Rethymno,** staying just one night in each place, then went 'home; to Agia Gallini, until it was time to go back to meet Helen back in Iraklion.

I met up with Helen, we took a boat back to stay in Athens a couple of days then flew back to the UK.

All in all, I enjoyed those few weeks.

Also, in the 1980's, I made a couple of journeys to **India**. The first was 1981, just a two week holiday on a houseboat and pony trekking in Kashmir with a friend called Lizzy.

The second was 1985, an eight week journey around North India, Nepal and Kashmir, with Lesley. I wrote about those times in my book

'BACK TO THE EAST, INDIA, NEPAL AND KASHMIR.'.

Also during the 80's, I took every opportunity to see my teacher, Maharaji. As well as places such as London, Brighton, Nottingham and Birmingham, I went to Rome three times, Brussels and Miami. Every time I found it to be an uplifting and refocussing experience.

Still in the 1980's whilst living at Waterloo Road, I flew to Rome and back a couple of times. On another occasion, friends Pete and Lisa who had a coach converted to live in, invited me to join a group of Premies and others that were going to Rome. It wasn't until after we left that I realised that most people had very little money. We were a mixed bunch of men and women with two children. I spent a lot of time up front with Pete who was doing almost all the driving; in fact I don't remember anyone else driving at all. I was keeping him on route and keeping him awake, down through France fr through Paris Lyons and on to Florence and then Rome

Pete Arnold

After the festival had ended and we were ready to head off back to Norwich, Pete announced that he did not have enough money to pay for the fuel to get us back to Norwich and apparently neither did anyone else.

I came up with the idea of sending the girls into the airport to ask the many Premies that were flying to their own homes, for financial assistance. Even I was surprised that it took them just a couple of hours to get the money we needed.

During the 1970's and 1980's, I attended several medieval-themed fairs in NOrfolk, the first being Barsham Fair in 1975 and 1976. I camped at both. There were lots of stalls selling craftwork and food and an excellent fireworks display. It was a tremendous atmosphere with plenty of people that I knew from Norwich. Also people were staying in converted coaches and trucks as well as horse-drawn wagons. In 1982, it was the time for Rougham Tree Fairs, much larger with more bands, more converted coaches, a lot more people and a lot more drugs.

A group of entertainers called the Tibetan Ukranian Mountain Troupe turned up on their coaches. I remember one day sitting on one of their coaches when a girl came in with a large hash cake. She cut it in half and into slices so that the dozen or so of us sitting there had a piece each. Then she cut the other half into two pieces, sliced one piece and handed everyone another slice, now half the size. This was repeated until the pieces were quite small! It was quite strong cake –

lovely. We were all stoned. Chillums were being passed around too. Somebody asked "was there acid in that cake?" "Of course," said the girl, "there's acid in all our food". Of course, there wasn't.

I met a chap that was to become a good friend at those fairs; we called him Tibetan Tom, even though he wasn't Tibetan.

"Tibetan" Tom

There were plenty of other fairs, such as at East Berholdt in Suffolk in 1981, the Blue Moon Fair in Nenthead, Cumbria in 1982, where we had so much rain that vehicles had to be pulled out of the field by tractor. At that fair, I ran a stall selling fried egg sandwiches, egg fried rice, veggie burgers and extremely strong spirit coffees – and hash cakes. Polish Chris (Chris Lausch) and Mark Angus helped me. We called it the 'Whirling Pit'.

Another event was the Norwich Free Festival at Eaton Mill, on the outskirts of the City. People had to go through the double-gated railway crossing to get there. The site, which was on disputed land, included a pool where people swam and played, naked, and there were plenty of naked people wandering around, cheap food and lots of drugs. I was laying on my back in the sunshine with my eyes closed and I hear a voice saying "Do you want some hash cake?" When I opened my eyes all I saw was mass of black pubic hair belonging to a girl crouching down, almost sitting on my face!

There was also an earth pipe. One had to lay down and suck on a mouthpiece that came out of the ground; the bowl was lit at the other end of a channel that had been cut out and covered, several feet away.

By this time the 'Peace Convoy' consisting of an increasing number of coaches and trucks were turning up at fairs. On the whole they were welcomed but a small number started stealing from local communities and earned them a bad name.

An old tradition at these 'Albion Fairs' was to hoist a flag, which by some ancient law, apparently, meant that the police could not legally enter the site unless chasing in a criminal or invited.

Mark Angus, Polish Chris and I had a stall there, again selling food and spirit coffees; rum, vodka, brandy. Our stall was opposite the stage where the bands played and off to our right was the main entrance. Behind us were two rows of vehicles belonging to the Peace Convoy.

On the day after the Fair ended, the flag was taken down and suddenly dozens of police in riot gear rushed in and lined up right in front of our stall, just about thirty feet away. I thought we were going to get battered.

Suddenly they rushed forwards towards us but they completely ignored us, split into two groups and rushed down to confront several dozen people that were part of the Convoy.

There was a stand off, fortunately, and negotiations. Apparently somebody had stolen a car and driven it on to the site and they wanted it back. Somebody in the convoy found the car, it was handed over and the police left with no further worry or trouble being caused.

These festivals, some for which one had to pay and entrance and camping fee and some of which were free, became a great gathering of souls from Norwich and elsewhere.

I used to stay in a small tent which was quite adequate.

There were plenty of food stalls but also some people with no money. One time somebody put a very large pot of water over an open fire, calling it 'Stone Soup'. It had two pebbles in it and people were invited to add ingredients, some opinions, potatoes, carrots, pulses, spices and so on. After a while it turned into a great spicy vegetable stew and the pebbles were removed and many people few!

Another regular attendee at many fairs and festivals was Pete Arnold and Lisa, along with his converted coach and wooden prefabricated pyramid which served as a living room and gathering point. He became known as 'Pyramid Pete', for a while.

In 1985, after returning from India with lots of goods to sell, Lesley helped me run a stall at Lyng Fair, Stanley was there too. That attracted the attention of the Norwich drugs squad and we were raided at Waterloo Road, twice in two weeks. They were looking for acid, they said. They found hash.

Stanley Atkins outside Waterloo Road

Also some time in the early 80's, I went with John and Kit Adam whom I stayed with back in 1973, to the South of France.

John drove down and we soon found ourselves along the Riviera with no place to stay, just the car and my little tent. Their daughter Carla who was about five was with us. As John drove from Cannes towards and passed St Tropez, we saw that all the camp sites and caravan parks had signed displayed saying "Complet", meaning full.

Suddenly, I spotted what looked like a large garden with tents and campers so we headed there. I saw a lady who looked like she was in charge and risked my French, saying "Est-il possible de camper ici?"

A younger woman that was with her asked in English how many people. I said "Trois persons et une enfante."

They let us stay. Apparently she had turned away several people that day and it was my attempt at French that won us a place. The beach of **Saint Claire** was right next to the beach and an ice cream stall and restaurant.

Kit, Carla and John Adam

In 1986, my friend Paddy had been living on his coach in Spain, close to Fuengirola, and my lodger went down to visit him. When he came back, he persuaded me to

106

join him of his own coach which he had just bought and head down to Spain.

My first trip there, however, was with Lesley. We flew to Malaga then took buses down the coast, visiting Gibraltar and a few other places, then to Fuengirola where we met up with Paddy.

After returning to Norwich, I agreed to go back to Spain with Stanley. He also invited two other friends, Steve and Cleo, which was not the best of ideas as they had been a couple and recently split up and neither knew the other was going until the day we left.

Cleo

Anyway I took a small tent and went we arrived and found Paddy's camp, I slept in that. We also spent some time parked up in the area near the Castle in **Fuengirola**.

I spent a week travelling to **Ibiza** and **Formentera** with

Cleo visiting Michael and Petra who had moved there from Norwich, travelling by train. Ibiza was out of season and very boring; San Antonio was horrid. Formentera was pleasant just to stroll around.

I met some great English people there, Patrick and Kate, Julia and Amanda, also some Germans called Jonnie, Harold the Baker and Norbert and his wife Claudia.

I stayed a few weeks and went back to Norwich, then flew down again with Lesley.

Lesley and I stayed in Jonnie's little house, "Rancho Tranquillo", a two mile walk into the 'campo,; which used car batteries for electricity and water from a nearby well.

It was actually a pleasant stroll down to the little town of La Cala with its delightful little bar where we were always welcomed with a large milky coffee which they called "Un Grande Andande" or 'Big Walk.'

German Jonnie

Harold The Baker

Rancho Tranquilo

Later we stayed with in an an apartment in **Calahonda**, with Patrick and Kate and Patrick's father Maurice, who was recovering from a stroke. There was also a Spanish guy called Carlos, that did not help things.

Patrick, Kate and Maurice at Calahonda

I was suffering then from what turned out to be duodenal ulcers. Everyone at Calahonda was drinking too much alcohol, Lesley included, and as it make my stomach hurt, I was abstaining. It resulted in a lot of arguments. There was also a Spanish guy from Madrid, called Carlos, who did not help and he kept bringing more alcohol.

One day Lesley stormed out and did not come back. I became worried, wondering where she was. I thought maybe she had gone to Fuengirola so I took a bus to look for her. When I got out of the bus, something made me walk to the beach. There she was! She was very drunk and the contents of her bag, her passport and money were scattered on the sand.

It turned out she had not been long sitting there. I got her stuff together and somehow got her back to Calahonda.

Lesley flew back to the UK but I stayed on.

Fuengirola, Spain 1985

After a few months, a few people from Norwich tuned up on the Costa del Sol. One was mark Angus. Another was a guy called Colin and he bought a camper van from German Jonnie and invited me to travel to France with him, to visit some more friends from Norwich, Smiley and Dalia, who were living on a farm for a while.

C

Mark Angus

111

Colin drove up to the French border where French customs thoroughly searched the van, even the chemical toilet. Funny thing was that I just sat outside the van with my rucksack and they completely ignored me.

We went to Toulouse where Fat Staley was parked in his concerted coach, under a bridge, stayed a few days then headed off to Saint-Pastour to stay with Smiley on the farm. They were looking after a farmhouse whilst the actual tenant was travelling. I spent hours sitting in the sunshine watching their chickens. They all had names. One was called Houdini as she constantly escaped.

Smiley

But I suffered there from duodenal ulcers and had to go

to the town hospital for an endoscope. That was not so pleasant but, hey, I survived.

Whilst staying there I met Spider, and English guy who had lived in the area some years with his French wife. Also Joe Thompson turned up in his converted truck, and Mick and Jane in theirs.

Stanley turned up for a day too and said he would pick me up and take me back to Norwich for Christmas. That did not work out.

Spider with Joe Thompson

I had phoned Sue in Norwich. She had agreed to go to Barbados if Stanley lost a couple of stone in weight. On the phone she asked me how Stanley was doing with losing weight and what he was eating. Without thinking but being honest, I said "The last thing I saw him eat in Toulouse was French custard tart."

Because of that, he did not pick me up, and suddenly Smiley's time at the farmhouse was over and I had to find somewhere to live; I did not have much money with me so Spider let me stay at his place until I organised a ticket on the train back to Norwich.

I stayed at Sue's house and took her to Amsterdam for new Year. Stanley did not like that and never spoke to me again.

I went back to Spain in 1988 and I stayed in a place called **Alhaurin El Grande** with Norbert, his wife Claudia who was suffering with MS and their daughter. Jessica. He was renting with a swimming pool house on an urbanisation just outside the town.

It was on a pleasant urbanisation just outside the town.

Claudia

I looked into buying a piece of land there and building a house. I did get as far as paying some money but one thing led to another and after I was busted and banged up in 1991, I lost the lot.

Jessica, Norbert, Claudia, Alan and Myself

My friend from Norwich, also flew out to join us. There was an element of competition between Alan and Norbert, who was best at tennis, who was best at backgammon, but that was OK, although I never knew whether they actually liked each other.

The group of myself, Norbert, Patrick and Kate, went to Tenerife. Alan flew out from the UK to meet us a few weeks later. When I got there, I received a message that Patrick and Kate were staying in a cave.

I was in **Los Cristianos** in a hotel. That was much smaller and more pleasant in those days than now, in 2021. So I took a bus with my suitcase and went to join them. Kate tells the story of how she was looking out of their cave and they saw me coming over the hill, dragging my suitcase.

Kate in the cave.

Tenerife was great. I went with Norbert and Alan for a trip in the yellow submarine. I did panic a little as it submerged, until I was told that the water pressure made the seal.

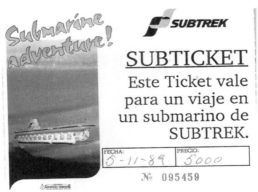

We didn't see much, an old bicycle, some drinks cans, but it otherwise looked as if we were flying over the surface of the moon.

Kate, Patrick, Norbert and myself, went to **La Gomera**, a fascinating small Island in the Canary Isle group, only a few miles across but with five climates.

We took a ferry and crossed the island, up through the rainforest and down the other side where we rented an apartment for a few weeks.

As we drove up from our apartment in La Caleta, we left behind cacti, bananas trees and palm trees, passed through an area of apple and orange trees, then gorse bushes, then Fir trees and finally into the rain forest.

On the beach one wore swimming costumes or shorts, at the top raincoats, hats and scarves. Almost all the rain on the island was at the top..

Valley Gran Rei, La Gomera

The area between the high cliffs and the sea is quite narrow and not suited for people that suffer from claustrophobia, I was told. I loved it.

.

I must say that I had a great time in Tenerife and vowed to go back

In 1988, I was lucky to get tickets and Hester and I went to **Wembley** Stadium to see **Pink Floyd**; it was an excellent gig.

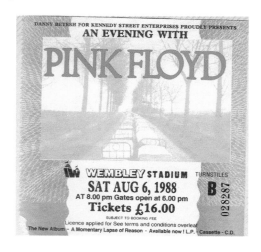

In 1989, I managed to get a good deal on flight and hotel in Miami, for a three day festival with my teachers, Maharaji.

I went with another premie, Beryl and a few days later her partner Mark joined us. We stayed in the Thunderbird hotel. They would not take cash and it was lucky that I had a credit card.

The Thunderbird was said to have the best Chinese restaurant in Miami. The food was very food. They served it at much lower prices in the hotel restaurants for guests only.

Miami

Most of the restaurants in **Miami** prided themselves in serving so much food that diners were able to take some home in a 'doggy bag.

One day in the hotel lobby, Beryl and I were standing waiting for Mark and Beryl started coughing. I heard a voice, that I recognised, saying "That's a nasty cough."

I turned around and indeed who I though it was. It was the actor and stand-up comedian **George Burns**. Younger people may not know who he was. He was famous for standing on stage, smoking a cigar, well into his nineties. He also played God in films such as 'Oh God', a popular 1977 film. He had been to the Chinese restaurant and, sure enough, was holding a doggy bag.

We saw brown pelicans flying past from our hotel balcony.

Miami was so humid that when I went outside or got out of the air-conditioned bus, my spectacles steamed up as if I was walking into a bathroom.

Mark with myself and Beryl Jackson

One day I decided to get something to eat for dinner outside the hotel. There was a diner across the road, so I went there. I had turkey drumstick and chips. There was masses and almost as soon as I started to eat, I just lost my appetite. I apologised to the waitress. She said she would wrap in up so I could take it away. I said that was no good as I was I a hotel. She brought a bag a bread rolls, saying I had to walk out with something or they'd get a bad name.

I crossed the road and went to the Thunderbird. Outside there were police cars. As I entered the foyer, somebody said "There he is!"

I thought 'whatever have I done?'

The cop asked where I had been. I told him. He said that reception staff saw me leave the hotel but I did not get into a taxi, I just walked. When they went outside to look for me, I had disappeared. He said that it was not safe to walk about in the evening; people could shoot me from a car! I should have taken a taxi. It was a dual carriageway and two miles either way before one could turn round, so going to that restaurant by taxi would have been a round trip of eight miles!

The event with Maharaji was wonderful. It was so uplifting. I felt safe in Miami, walked around part of the city, went to the beach for a fireworks display. All the girls serving in cafes and bars were beautiful but clearly over obsessed by their hair. Everyone seemed to me to be very friendly.

I went to the science museum. There I saw the outfits worn by astronauts. It was remarkably thin, consisting of a few layers of plastic, silver foil and hemp!

There was an exhibition called 'Walk on Mars'. For a price one could enter a room, walk up some steps, cross and platform and down some other steps. Set into the platform was a small glass case containing, supposedly, a small piece of a meteorite believed to have originated on Mars. I was given a certificate to say that I had walked on Mars!

In 1990, I went with my friend Alan to France, to taste some wine.

We rapidly drove (well Alan did) down to **Beaune**, a walled city in the Burgundy region, and found a hotel right in the centre, with a good restaurant and wine. By this time in my life, I was eating fish and birds again, just not four-legged creatures, so I had a delicious duck dinner. In fact, in all the time we were in France, maybe eight days, I must have eaten duck at least ten times, with all sorts of sauces, even duck souffle,

We visited the town of **Gevry Chambertin**, where we found a small restaurant with a wine cellar. I ordered coq au vin and Alan had boeuf bourguignon. We had to wait some time for our meal as it was cooked individually and by the time it had arrived, we had already drunk two bottles of fine wine. When the meal came it was fantastic, almost bright purple. The residue from aged vintage wines was used in the sauces. Afterwards we went down to the cellar and spent about £200 on six or seven bottles!

My travels did not stop there. I went to Egypt twice, the first time with Sue in 1989 and the second time with Lesley in 1990. Although I wrote the book as a semi-fiction with time travel back to 2000 BC, the first part reflects those two journeys. Based once again on the 'Hat' narrator theme, I called it

'MYHAT IN EGYPT THROUGH THE EYES OF A GOD'.

In 1991, I was busted for conspiracy to import and conspiracy to supply cannabis and in 1992 given two concurrent ten year prison sentences. That story I have told in yet another book:

'TIME FOR CANNABIS THE PRISON YEARS'.

I served four and a half years of that sentence, firstly over twelve months of remand, the, after conviction, ten months in a maximum security prison due to the length of the sentence, Whitemoor; from there I went to HMP Blantyre House in Kent, a unique C Category prison where inmates and screws alike wore their own clothes. The Governor, Jim Semple, had the idea that many inmates serving long sentences did not deserve or need the strict, limiting and soul-destroying regimes of maximum security prisons. At HMP Whitemoor, they had a good computer department so I learned to work with word processing, databases and spreadsheets. I passed the exams and applied for and won a place with the Open University studying Fundamentals of Computing. The rest of my days there, I spent playing bridge or reading; I built a database on the Egyptian Pharaohs, monuments and tombs. That concluded with the publishing of what was actually my first book:

'FROM DOT TO CLEOPATRA, A CONCISE HISTORY OF ANCIENT EGYPT'.

In Whitemoor, I met guys that I would never have met anywhere else. Often they were seemingly decent people considering their crimes; there were heroin and cocaine smugglers, armed robbers, killers and even a terrorist or two. As I said though, the story of those years is in another book.

Whilst at **HMP Blantyre House**, the prison governor **Jim Semple** (who always said "Don't call me Sir") approached myself and my friend Will Hutchinson, who I had been in Norwich and Whitemoor prisons and who was also on a course of study, and asked us if we would help him with a survey amongst our fellow inmates. He had devised a series of questions in an attempt to compare what he called the "Prison Experience" between their previous prison and Blantyre House. The House had just over a hundred inmates, almost all of whom were serving at least six years and had completed at least third of it without getting into trouble; there were a lot of drugs smugglers, some in for heavy fraud, even armed robbery or manslaughter. It was one of the few prisons, as Jim said, that actually told you the rules: they were no drugs or alcohol, no violence or verbal abuse and to commit oneself to at least half a day per week in education. In return we were trusted. We could wear our own clothes, go for countryside rambles on a Saturday, have more visits, go out for work or study and get more visits, eventually town visits (where we could go out for the day with family or friends, as far as

Hastings) and eventually home visits. Any rule-breakers were immediately shipped out, back to a more secure prison such as Swaliside or Whitemoor, where they had come from.

Whilst there I kept myself busy with my Open University course, making my database on Egypt, taking classes such as Spanish and German, but also joined the 'Amenities Committee' which liaised between inmates and staff, trying to get more and more amenities. I joined the indoor bowls team and took part in the pantomime. I also helped organise two '**Stir Crazy**' days, when over a thousand people and carers from **Mencap** came into the prison grounds for a day of food, races, clowns, stalls, games with prizes, bands and fun. It was all manned by inmates organised by myself and one of the best screws, Mick Pallant.

Mick Pallant

The second time I negotiated so that the inmates could

wear fancy dress, which we did. It was tremendous experience; the Mencap disadvantaged were so caring of each other. They were aged from about fifteen to seventy. We also had to raise the funds and book the bands. I formed a group called 'CAGE', the Charities Action Group Enterprise, raising funds for Mencap, Gingerbread and Victim Support charities. I wrote monthly quiz sheets and even ran a couple of 'Clever Coffee Evenings', like a pub quiz without booze.

Jim even drove Will Hutchinson and I to the Cambridge Institute of Criminology to do a presentation before judges, prison governors, police and barristers as well as criminology students. Jim was so pleased that he even took us for a pint of beer on the way back, swearing us to secrecy (well that was over twenty five years ago..

Will Hutchinson, Jim Semple and myself at
The Cambridge Institute of Criminology

All that got me plenty of praise and appreciation,

apparently earning the prison such good points that they decided to refuse me parole and keep me there for another year!

Will and I did the survey and afterwards wrote a report based on the results. Years later I published it on Amazon; it is called:

DAMAGE AND HUMANITY IN CUSTODY.

A few months before what was to be my parole date, Ralph from the education department called me in and said I had done so much that they wanted to do something back for me and offered me free driving lessons. I had about twenty lessons and was just about to take my test when I was given parole and thrown out on to the street. Well,, not actually on the street as I had somewhere to stay, at the house owned by Sue whom I had been to Egypt with in 1989.

Sue was living with her partner, Mike. I stayed for a few months then took a room in a house owned by Hester, for a few more months, in Helena Road.

I was on parole and had to go along to the office once a week, then once a fortnight, then once a month, for about a year. I made sure, out of principle, to be on time and polite. My parole officer, Sue Upton, was good lady and understood and accepted my political campaign against the cannabis laws, providing, she said, that I didn't smoke or deal it. I decided it was best to hide all that from her. I know I was not addicted, but I did like a smoke. During my four and a half years incarcerated, I went without a smoke for only about four days. Even in

Whitemoor, a maximum security prison, one could get some hash in. I just enjoyed it and it did no harm to anyone and, as I write this in reasonable health at seventy one years old, maybe it did me no harm either.

My problem was what to do. I could not continue with my Open University computer studies because I had no computer. I applied for jobs but prison was the barrier. I went to NACRO (the National Association for the Care and Resettlement of Offenders), but they said they could not help as I was already too qualified. So I signed on the dole.

By then I was going back to Jack's Yard almost every day, helping him with his campaign to 'Campaign to Legalise Cannabis International Association' or 'CLCIA', which I had helped found in 1991, whilst on bail. It was now late 1996.

A few months later, I went to a cannabis conference in London and met **Howard Marks**, who had not long been released from prison in the US. That story is in his book 'Mr Nice' where he mentions visiting Norwich to get the passport from Donny Nice. Howard did not mention me in the book, but he did remember meeting me at that garden flat in1976.

We asked Howard if he would stand for Parliament on the cannabis issue and he said yes, and a whole new episode in my life opened up.

I decided to rent my own place and found a two-bedroomed house in Winter Road, Norwich, thinking that if Howard Marks needed somewhere to stay during his election campaign, he could stay there.

As it happened, he stayed at the Maids Head Hotel when he was in Norwich. I persuaded him to appoint Derek Williams as his election agent, to attempt to seal the rift that had developed between Derek, a campaigner in his own right, and many in the local cannabis campaign community. It was not such a good move as Derek was very anti-tobacco and wanted to make it part of Howard's campaign, but Howard did not agree. Howard received about 600 votes in each of Norwich South and Norwich North, about 1.6%. He was disappointed but we were pleased. It was at the Hustings at Norwich City College, when Derek asked the panel of candidates who had taken cannabis. Of course Howard said yes, as did the Green Party candidate, Adrian Holmes, but the big surprise was that Labour candidate Charles Clarke also said he had tried it as a student in the US.

Howard Marks. Election campaigns helped bring the issue into the political arena and led to the formation of the first ever UK cannabis-focussed political party in1999.

Lesley, Howard, Tina and Jack

Alun Buffry & Howard Marks, Norwich, 1997

Also in 1997, as Melissa, my God-daughter and the daughter of Judi, was now sixteen and wanted to leave home, I rented a room to her at Winter Road.

During my stay there, the drugs squad turned up. They climbed through the kitchen window. I heard them coming up the stairs. I was still in bed, reading 'Trainspotting'. They searched the house. They said that they were there, along with police from the Devon and Cornwall force, because I had been writing to a guy in prison who was inside for cultivating cannabis and he mentioned it is his letters as if he wanted me to grow it. They left disappointed.

Also, whilst I was living in Winter Road, there, Jack and a few others formed what they called UCHASH, the **Universal Church of the Holy and Sacred Herb**. They held a smoking protest in the cloisters of Norwich Cathedral, telling the Bishop of Norwich in advance, gathered one day on the grass and lit and passed around a chillum, that actually contained lavender. I wasn't there, but Melissa was, and that evening I saw on TV how the police had hidden around the cloisters, then 'pounced.' I saw them take Melissa to search her and a few others. Jack had cannabis in his pocket so was arrested.

I decided to lodge a complaint against the police for interfering in a religious ritual, so wrote a letter. I tried to encourage Jack and the others to do the same.

A few weeks later there was a knock on the door. It was a man from the Police Complaints Department, about my letter. I explained that although that UCHASH was no more part of my beliefs than the Cathedral's version of Christianity, I did believe that people had the Human Right to choose and practice their own beliefs and that I thought police had acted unnecessarily. I said that a chillum was part of their religion and showed him my collection; I said I have many Buddha's too, but I am not a Buddhist. He said that I was the only person in the country that had complained about it. So, I said in that case I will drop the complaint.

I moved to Mornington Road, in Norwich, and Melissa moved too.

Whilst living there, I initiated a case against the British Government in the European Court of Human Rights, over their interference without good reason, with the belief that consumption of cannabis was good for them. I collected over 600 statements from people, but had no legal representation due to lack of funds. Several months later it was thrown out at the administrative level, so never went to the court itself; they said there was no appeal process and they did not have to give reasons.

In 1999, Jack Girling and I officially registered the **'Legalise Cannabis Alliance** (LCA)' as a political party. I became the Nominating Officer and National Coordinator, whose job is to officially authorise candidates to use the part name and emblem. Jack was put as leader although we made it clear to the Elections Committee that it was "for the purposes of registration only." We did not want a party leader. We wanted a single-issue, cannabis-focussed, party with independent candidates that couple express their own views on other issues.

By that time, Jack's scrap yard, which he'd used as the base for his campaign, also a wood yard, burned down and Jack was living in his mother's house in Peacock Street.

One day Jack said we should have a conference for the

LCA, so I booked a room in Wensum Lodge in Kings Street, Norwich. After a while I went to see Jack and asked what he was doing to promote the conference. "Nothing", he said, "We should leave it up to the Lord."

I said I thought that God was supposed to help those that helped themselves and that leaving it up to the Lord may be why we were in such a mess in the world today.

The room was full of smoke and Jack stood up and went to open the door, then asking the six or seven people there to leave. Then he came and grabbed me by my shirt and told me to get out. I left. I have never been inside anywhere that Jack lived, although I still let him into my house. By then I had moved again, into the rented house where I still live, twenty years later, in Woodcock Road. I am sad to say that he often turned up late at night, talking about what God had supposedly said to him. I never really knew what he was going on about. For me he is entitled to his beliefs and religion but I don't need to be preached to. By the time he left, often at 2 am, I was wound up. So in fact I felt better off without him. I became the Party Leader, again in name only, as well as National Coordinator and Nominating Officer.

We had our first LCA party conference, it was a great success with about a hundred in attendance and Howard Marks as guest speaker. I was not sure The Lord did much to help though.

We had a couple of candidates in parliamentary by-elections: the ex-labour Mayor of Carlisle, Colin Paisley stood in Kensington and Chelsea against Michael Portillo. Derek Large stood in Romsey.

In 2001, LCA had thirteen candidates in the General Election. I stood in Norwich South, against Charles Clarke.

That was again a whole new experience for me; not just designing fliers but doing interviews with the local press and radio station and attending Hustings alongside career politicians.

At Hustings, I had to answer questions on subjects such as education, the problem with administration at the colleges, pollution on the Norwich ring road, pensioners and even immigration. I found I could bring cannabis to many issues. I was also aware that **Charles Clarke** was listening closely. I did notice that he liked to drink.

At the Hustings at UEA, we were invited for a sherry beforehand, in the Union Presidents office. Charles was there with his wife. He got up and picked up two glasses of sherry. As he sat down, he said something to his wife (well I assume it was his wife, it may have been his election agent). She stood up and went and picked up two more glasses of Sherry,

Received of MR. A. BUFFRY
the sum of FIVE HUNDRED Pounds
Shillings Pence
DEPOSIT AS A CANDIDATE
£ 500 — 00
21 MAY 2001

Our party manifesto was called :

135

'CANNABIS; LEGALISE AND UTILISE.'

Alun Buffry LCA versus Charles Clarke, 2001

AALDERS-DUNTHORNE
Andrew Paul Aalders-Dunthorne
Ashfield House,Ashfield Green,Stradbrooke,Harleston,Norfolk.IP21 5NL
Liberal Democrat

BUFFRY
Alun Buffry commonly known as Alsie Buffry
203 Woodcock Road, Norwich, Norfolk, NR3 3TG
Legalise Cannabis Alliance

CLARKE
Charles Rodway Clarke
66 Eaton Road, Norwich, NR4 6PR
The Labour Party Candidate

FRENCH
Andrew John French
15 Grove Avenue, Norwich, Norfolk, NR1 2QB
The Conservative Party Candidate

HOLMES
Adrian St. John Holmes
163 Oak Street, Norwich, NR3 3AY
The Green Party Candidate

MANNINGHAM
Edward David Manningham
7 The Grove, Woodcock Road, Norwich, Norfolk, NR3 3TN
Socialist Alliance

MILLS
Tarquin Alexander Graham Mills
21 Rowington Road, Norwich, Norfolk, NR1 3RR
U.K. Independence Party Candidate

I received over 700 votes about 1.6%, which I was pleased with.

LCA had over eighty candidates in various elections between 1999 and 2006. We distributed almost a million fliers, had a party broadcast on TV in Wales, and radio and TV throughout Britain.

In 2001, I testified before the Home Affairs Select Committee, debated at the Oxford Union and participated in numerous TV and radio interviews and all with no previous experience and on s show-string budget.

That story is told in yet another book:

OUT OF JOINT, 20 YEARS OF CAMPAIGNING FOR CANNABIS.

In 2002, I went with Judi to the university of Wales, **Lampeter**, to attend he daughter and my Go-daughter Melissa's graduation ceremony. After studying there for three years, Melissa was awarded a BA in Anthropology and Religion. Despite not having attended my own graduation ceremony in 1971, I was pleased that she agreed to attend, so hired for he a mortarboard and town.

We were both very proud of her. Lampeter was a small town in Ceredigion, so small that the population tripled when the students were there. We visited Aberystwyth while we were there

After graduating, Melissa came back to Norwich and took a few short jobs before starting a course in teaching at the University Of East Anglia and found a room in a flat for that time, then moved into my spare room. She decided to cycle around some parts of Europe and managed to get some grants to help pay he expenses, also intending to work on some work-for-keep farms and do some teaching. One of the places she was going to was Helsinki. She told me that she had applied to cross the border into Russia and do some teaching there. A couple of days later it was April 1st and I could not resist a joke. I knocked on her bedroom door and said "Melissa, there's a couple of Russian policemen downstairs want to talk to you about working in Russia." "Oh, that was quick," she said. I could hardly stop myself laughing out loud as I led her downstairs, opened the kitchen door and said "Here she is officers".

Whilst Melissa was in **Helsinki**, she invited us to go there for Christmas as she had the use of an apartment used by her friend James, who was not there. Lesley, Judi and myself flew to Tampere airport. The days were short and it was damned old. The apartment was adequate but our mobile (cell) phones would not find a signal inside, which was a surprise since Nokia originated there. Helsinki was also where Melissa met her future husband, Matteo.

Also, in 2002, I worked on a project with Don Barnard, a document with information and logical arguments that we could present to the MP's. We even had one printed in Braille, for David Blunkett, the then Home Secretary. We sent a copy to every MP. Although we did not end up changing the law, we did see cannabis temporarily down-graded, which, I was told by an MP, was much to do with the LCA and this document. It was called:

CANNABIS; CHALLENGING THE CRIMINAL JUSTICE SYSTEM

Don Barnard and myself

So from 1999 to 2006, I was busy running the Party.

After that LCA became a pressure group and I was still involved until 2011. That did not mean I did not travel, although I would say the journeys were holidays rather than expeditions. I travelled a lot with Lesley. That included Italy, Spain, Portugal, Switzerland, Holland, France, Belgium, Germany, Finland, The Czech Republic, Hungary, Romania, Tunisia and several times to Tenerife.

In 2000, I went to the Hemp Parade in **Berlin**, along with Lesley, Melissa and Ann Clark RIP) and met with an online friend, Miro (RIP). We flew from Stansted.

Miro, Lesley, myself and Melissa, outside the Berlin
Hemp Museum, which was closed.

I produced a book which shows photographs of many
places I visited, called

AND THERE I WAS.

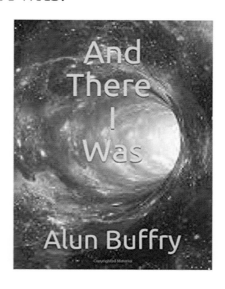

In 2001, I had the honour of escorting my God-daughter, Melissa, To Italy to attend events with Maharaji in Rome and then on to Switzerland where he was due to speak in Geneva. We flew to Rome and stayed in a hotel in the centre. We had the opportunity to visit the Colosseum and the Vatican. Listening to Maharaji is always an uplifting experience. We went by train, then, to Florence, for a few days and from there to Geneva, again by train.

When we were in **Florence**, we went for a meal in a tiny restaurant next to the wonderful Cathedral of Santa Maria del Flore. Just after finishing our excellent meal there was a massive clash of thunder and a flash on lightning, which must have hit to Dome. All the lights went out. We were quickly supplied with candles and then torrential rain. Whilst we sipped limoncello and then coffee, I though we are going to get soaked. There I was in sandals (and socks), jeans and shirt, no coat or umbrella and no hat. It was too far to walk without getting soaked and too close to justify a taxi.

I said a little prayer – please rain, stop so we can get to the hotel.

Almost instantly the rain stopped. We quickly left and walked the ten minutes or so to our hotel. Just as we went inside, the downpour started again.. It lasted for hours!

I very much enjoyed Florence and so, a couple of years later, I went back with Lesley, for a holiday. We saw all the sites, crossed the bridge where all the goldsmiths trade and spent some hours in the market.

Florence

Geneva

One evening, after a meal of gnocchi, which I did not enjoy, and a bottle of wine, Lesley and I were walking

143

back to our hotel behind the train station. There was a guy in the street that just came and stood directly in front of me. I stopped, I moved to one side and he also stepped aside so he was still in front of me. He asked for a cigarette, I said I did not smoke. Then he stood besides me and sort of put his bent leg in front of me. Then I felt his arm behind my back and his hand trying to get into my pocket on my other side. I just pushed him slightly and we walked on. That was the end of that. Lesley, however, once we were in our room started saying how outrageous and dangerous that guy could be and we should report him to the police. I said he was probably gone now, but she said we should tell the hotel management. I said I would go to look and see if he was still there (remember I had drank most of a bottle of wine and several limoncellos). She said not to as he may attack you. I said "I'll take a knife.." I didn't go though.

In 2002, Lesley and I thought we could maybe get a cheap holiday in Luxor. There was a notice for one in a travel agent's window in Norwich, so we went in to ask about it. Unfortunately they had sold out, but they offered us a cheap holiday in **Hammemet** in **Tunisia**, flight and accommodation in a three star hotel. We booked it.

A few weeks later we were standing in the immigration passport queue at the airport. I heard a voice behind us saying "Alun!".

I turned around and saw my old mate Tommy and his wife Georgie, whom I had not seen for probably twenty years, even though we lived in the same city. It turned out that they had been in the same travel agents and bought the same holiday probably an hour after us! They were in a different hotel but we did meet up on a couple of trips, one to an evening of food and belly dancing and another for along bus ride to a show, a meal and half an hour in a casino.

The casino trip was strange. First there was show with a juggler, a magician and a Robbie Williams lookalike, followed by a chicken and chips meal, then ten pounds each free chips for the casino (not bad considering the whole evening was just fifteen pounds each). They told us that we could only stay there for half an hour so we did not have to risk losing too much money.

We went in to the bright, glittery place and were given

tokens for the bandit machines. I rapidly lost all of mine. Lesley won quite a few tokens. She changed her tokens for chips to try roulette. She immediately put one chip on a number and lost it. I said try betting on a block or odds and evens, or black and red. No, she put another chip on another number. Now she only had one chip left. She put it on a colour and won. Then she put the now two chips on the same colour and lost.

So that was that. Then we found out that the chips were two at twenty pounds each and one at ten!

When we were back on the bus, the tour guide asked if anyone had won. One chap at the back of the bus said yes, he and his wife had won ten pounds each. They had taken the tokens and cashed them in. They had not played anything.

One day when we woke up, Lesley's arm was black and blue. It looked really bad, so I called for a doctor.

The doctor said she would have to go into hospital in case she was damaged inside her body. So they took her off in an ambulance. She was kept in overnight and they did X-rays. Holiday insurance covered the cost. I went a couple of times by taxi, the next day, then she was back in the hotel.

There was some English girls there and they asked if she was OK. I said yes but they did X-rays in case she was damaged inside, but I had wondered why. They said that they thought the doctor may have thought I'd beaten her, which was, they said, normal in Tunisia and nota crime!

One day, whilst sitting round the hotel swimming pool, we met a lady who chatted to us and asked Lesley if I had hit her. She said no and the lady said that I did not look that type. She told us she was there after a month in Egypt and was about to go on a cruise. A week after we were back in Norwich we happened to see her on TV in a programme about lottery winners.

Hammemet was out of season so not many tourists about, so when we went to the tourist Medina, all the salesmen wanted to sell us something. It was not actually a pleasant experience at all.

By now, 2004, I was getting the travellers bug. I read that there was a wine and folk festival in **Budapest** in September. Lesley said it was too far to go but I showed her on a map it is actually closer than Malaga or Tunisia. I was very excited about going to Hungary. We flew there direct from Stansted. We booked a room in a cheap hotel called Marco Polo, within walking distance of the centre. After eating masses of Hungarian food we headed down to the Danube and Chain Bridge. Actually a lot of Hungarian food such as goulash is meat orientated but we easily found fish.

The bridge was very beautifully lit that evening. We didn't cross it at that point.

Budapest is a city consisting of two cities, Buda, where we were, and Pest, across the river, where the Castle was and where the wine festival was t be held and also the Children's Railway. The impressive Hungarian Parliament buildings, main station and the more commercial areas are on the Buda side.

The folk and wine festival was fun. There were groups of wine makers that came down from the hills, all dressed in their local costumes and some dancing in the square in the castle district.

Also in this area is the Fisherman's Bastion

From here one has a beautiful view of the Parliament buildings across the Danube.

A few days later, we went back to the Castle to visit the strange labyrinths below the castle. One could easily get lost in the badly lit tunnels, which are scattered with random images and structures, including what is supposed to be (according to the notice in several languages) fossilised footprints from trainers and a computer keyboard, said to evidence of a human civilisation from millions of years ago, called Homo Consumus.

I was hard to see what some of the items were, until I looked at the photos I took with flash.

I would recommend that anyone visiting Budapest give the labyrinths a visit.

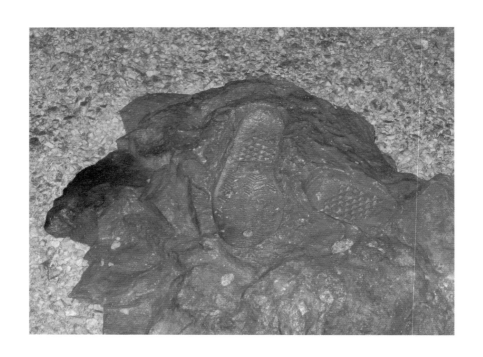

154

We spent another day trying out the Children's Railway. It is not a train set but a full size railway that one can ride, with trains driven by adults but young teenagers dressed in their uniforms manning the platforms. It runs on the Pest side up into the hills.

We were so impressed with Budapest that we decided to go back to the wine festival the following year, 2005.

I sorted the dates on line, booked the flights and a good Spa hotel near the river. We decided to go from there to **Romania**, so I booked the train tickets to and a room in Sighisoura, in Transylvania where Dracula Vlad Tepes was born, a stay in a 'mansion in the grounds of a castle', a hotel in Brasov and our flight home from Bucharest.

We arrived safely in Budapest at a splendid hotel with a lovely view of the river. I asked at reception about the wine festival, only to be told it was not that weekend but the weekend afterwards by which time we would be in Romania. The information on the internet had been wrong. Still, we were not too discouraged and had a good five days, before catching the train for the twelve our journey to Sighisoura.

By the time we got there, it was getting dark. We descended onto the platform. Although most people were going down steps to the subway at the other end of the platform there were steps closer to us, so we went down.

Yuk! It was like a cess pool with shit all over the floor. Stupidly I lifted the cases and trod warily through it, with Lesley holding her nose behind me. We exited and there was a beautiful little cottage with flowers in the garden, but I could not see where to go now. Just then a chap come out of the subway, dressed like a bank clerk or similar. I asked which was to the Citadel. He pointed back to the subway. We had come out the wrong side, we had to walk through it again.

When we finally got to the correct side, I spotted some men sitting on a wall and behind the wall were taxis. So, I approached them and said "Taxi?"

They shook their heads.

I pointed and again said "Taxi?".

They shook their heads again.

I shrugged and said "We want a taxi!"

One of the men shook his head and said "Yes, yes, Sit, we have taxis."

So this is like Turkey, I said to Lesley, shaking the head is saying yes, not nodding.

So we set off to our lovely room at the tiny Casa Wagner in the citadel area.

Sighisoura was a lovely place, at least in the Citadel area.

We stayed almost a week. There was not too much fuss over the Dracula theme but we did go to a restaurant that had, supposedly, once been the house where Vlad the Impaler had been born, drank bulls blood wine and ate blood coloured food. Also there was a small bust of Vlad nearby.

From there we went to the village "in the grounds of a castle". Well apparently a long time ago the Castle, which was sixty miles away, had huge grounds including where this village was., but nowadays one could not visit it. The family had been ousted but returned so the "count" was now trying to raise funds to repair the castle by renting rooms in this house. Two of our friends had come from Norwich to join us for a five day stay. The food that was included in the price, since there was nowhere else to eat in the village, was cooked by local girls who had, we were told, failed miserably at cooking English food, so they were told to cook as they would for guests in their homes. That meant lots of port stews which polenta with the same sauce for vegetarians. It was OK but monotonous. Pudding was windfall apples.

Whilst staying there we did go on a couple of day trips. One to a Saxon village where Prince Charles apparently owned a small house, to visit a church and once on a horse and cart ride, which was a bit rough. When we reached the destination on the edge of a woody area, I wandered around and started to find various mushrooms. I did not pick any. It was only when we were back in the "mansion" and I spotted an itinerary that I realised it was a mushroom spotting trip!"

Our next stop was **Brasov**. We caught a third class train that cost pennies. It was, we were told later, a "passenger train", meant for animals.

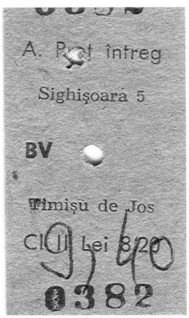

Brasov itself was quite a nice place. It was the base for skiing in the winter and one could take a day trip to **Bran Castle**, which had inspired Bram Stoker's Dracula story, although he never actually went there.

After leaving Brasov, we took a train to the west of Romania to a Saxon town called **Sibiu**. It was pleasant but nothing special. We stayed a few days then went by train to **Bucharest**, which was a big noisy city that neither us liked. We flew back to Stansted from there.

We were far from done with travelling yet and in 2005 we headed for Prague and the Czech Republic.

I was pick-pocketed in Prague on the crowded and packed Metro. I lost only £40 and a credit card which I stopped in time, but the zips on the jacket I was wearing were broken. I had to buy a new winter coat.

We visited **Kutna Hoar** with its Gothic Cathedral, olden coin mint and Ossuary, the small town of **Chesky Krumlov** with the UNESCO heritage centre, where we arrived in the middle of a blizzard. A nice place but very cold.

Cesky Krumlov

Next was **Ceske Budejovice** where they still make beers from the water of an underground lake, beer which eventually became Budweiser although not made with such unique water. We took the brewery tour and sampled fresh beer. It was very cold in both places.

In 2007, I went with Melissa and Lesley to Venice. By then Melissa was living in **Lu**, a small village in Northern Italy, with Matteo, her Italian partner, and was pregnant.

Venice was great. We stayed just outside and caught a bus each day across the long bridge to close to the train station. From there we could walk about or, if needed, catch a water bus on the Grand Canal. We visited San Marco Square and had to walk along planks as it was partly flooded. We had some excellent meals whilst we were in Venice. I would love to go back one day.

In 2009, we were back in Italy, this time visiting the beautiful Heritage site of **Bergamo**, on the way to stay with Melissa and Matteo in Lu Monferato. We flew direct to Bergamo, stayed a few days, went to Lu and back to Bergamo for a night before flying from there to Oporto, in Portugal. Those Ryan Air flights were so cheap.

Although we stayed in the lower and more modern busier part of Bergamo, we were able to walk to the funicular to go to the upper old town, which was lovely.

Porto, or Oporto, is one of my favourite places and we went there three time, the first being 2009. It was the added bonus of the port houses where one can book a tour and sample and buy port. I found it a very relaxing town, with its small streets and squares and excellent food served in really massive amounts.

Later in 2009, we journeyed to **Lucerne**, in Switzerland, which is now another one of my favourite cities We were lucky that it was warm. It was clean and friendly and has many attractions, ranging from the beautiful town centre and take, to the Natural History and Science museums, both well worth the visit. There is also a long covered wooden pedestrian bridge that has burned down and been repaired several times.

The **Dying Lion of Lucerne** is a fantastic rock carving hewn in about 1820 and commemorates the death of Swiss Guards in Paris during the French Revolution. It lies besides a small pond, trees and grass.

By 2009, I had been in touch with Paddy again. He had

been caught leaving Morocco on his coach with almost half a ton of cannabis, and banged up in a prison for many months, before being included in a Royal pardon. He told me how bad it was in there but made better if one had a somebody to bring in food, which his daughter did. One had to buy a mattress from the chief and when one left or died, the mattress went back to the chief again,

Paddy had contacts in the travel business and got us tickets to **Luxor**, that is for himself, Lesley and myself, sharing a bungalow on Kings Island at the Jolie Ville hotel, half board at a good price.

I wanted to go for my birthday, February 2nd, when it would not, hopefully, be too hot.

I was packed and ready to go when Paddy turned up at about 4 pm, in his car to drive us to Gatwick airport. Lesley, however, was at her own place, packing. I phoned her. She had three mobiles and a house phone. I had two numbers and her house phone number in my notebook. I tried them all, numerous times, with no answer. So about 5.30, Paddy said he'd drive to her house and knock on the door. Half an hour or so later, he was back, There had been no answer.

Lesley's other number was on my computer so I had to switch it on. I got the number. This was for an older phone she did not use often. I phoned it and she answered! I said I'd been trying her other numbers, she said "Oh, I've switched them off, I'm only taking my old one." I said Paddy had been knocking on her door. She said "Oh, I thought it was banging from next door."

So, not soon enough, we were on our way.

An hour or so into the drive, my phone rang. It was my niece in Barry in Wales. She said that Terry, my sister's partner, had a massive heart attack and died at Cardiff airport just after they had retuned from a holiday in Spain, He was just 55. What could I do? Even if I went straight to Wales, there was nothing I could do. Gwyneth was surrounded by family and friends. Also if I did not go to Luxor, it was doubtful that Paddy and Lesley would go. Well, I knew they wouldn't.

We arrived at our hotel about 11.30. There was nothing to eat except a delivery pizza. Mine tasted odd. I binned it. Paddy and Lesley both ate some of theirs and were feeling sick the next day.

But we arrived in Luxor and got the shuttle bus to our hotel without problem. It was a nice 25 degrees. Our bungalow in the grounds was superb, quiet in lovely gardens, three minutes walk from the Nile.

Paddy had brought a teapot. Every morning he was up

at 6 am and in the dining room, filling his pot with hot water with the tea he had brought, reading the English newspapers. I don't know what he had already eaten by the time I got there about 8. As for me, I had a hearty breakfast. Lovely creamy cold muesli like porridge, fruits, sliced turkey ham with cheese and a fried egg, pancakes, croissants and cakes! Lesley would drift in about 9.30 and have some cake!

Talking of food, the evening meals were also serve-oneself buffets and each evening, as well as staples such as pizza, fish and chips, burgers and kebabs and a whole range of salads, Egyptian food and cakes, there was a different themed dish: French, Italian, Chinese, Sushi, Oriental curries, English and Egyptian. Paddy and I ate masses. It showed.

As the week progressed, it became hotter and hotter. Three days after we arrived in was 28 degrees, Four days later it was 38 degrees, too hot to go far.

So we were lucky that by then we had seen some sites. I

had seen them before, as had Lesley, in 1990, but it was all new to Paddy although he wasn't as enthusiastic as us. We went to Luxor and **Karnak** temples and to the West Bank to see the **Mortuary Temple of Hatshepsut** and the **Ramasseum**.

The sunsets were impressive

It was a great two weeks, but all too soon we were landing back at Gatwick airport at midnight. It was minus 5 degrees. We took a taxi back to the hotel where we had stayed as they looked after the car for free for two weeks. Of course there was nobody at reception, but the keys were there. Paddy had to go down to the car park, without a torch, and find his car. I could here his swearing in the distance. He told me later that he kept putting his foot through frozen puddles.

We quickly loaded up and set off. Paddy had a hospital appointment a 9 am that morning. We headed towards the south circular road. The road eastwards was closed. We had to go round and join the north circular. The A10 and A11 were also closed. We had to take the A12. As soon as we reached it, we met very thick fog, all the way back to Norwich where it suddenly cleared. But it was then 6.30. Fortunately Paddy made his appointment on time.

2009 also had us visiting **Bilbao, Vitoria** and **Santiago de Compostela,** in Spain.

Also **Braga**, **Viana do Castelo** and **Porto** in Portugal.

Paddy had a house in France and we went to visit him in 2011. Whilst in the area we visited **Carcassonne**, a beautiful castle but very touristy, the beautiful lake caves at **Labouce** and the mysterious **Rennes Le Chateau.**

In 2011, the members of the Legalise Cannabis Alliance decided to elect a party leader. I had not formed the party to either be or follow a leader. I believed in local leaders. Even though the party had withdrawn its registration with the Electoral Commission and continued as a pressure group, I was against having a leader.

So after that was decided, I resigned from LCA. The new so-called leader changed the name, policy, literature, web site, took down the members' forum and even formed a new constitution. The party became unrecognisable. He rapidly lost the support of many or the candidates, formed a new committee and managed to alienate many of them too.

To be honest, I was glad to be out of it. LCA had suited its purpose and I was happy to be independent and speaking only for myself again.

In 2011, a Dutch Coffeeshop owner, **Nol Van Shaik**, invited Lesley and I to stay at his hillside complex near **Alora** in Spain, not far from Malaga and inland. I had met Nol at his coffeeshops in Haarlem in Holland, in about 2004 and retained contact and friendship with him and his lady, Maruska.

His place in Spain, which consisted of a house, several

apartments, a club house and a swimming pool, all fenced in and secured, was beautiful. The view across the little valley to the tiny village of **Las Mellizas** was one of the most splendid I had seen anywhere, especially when high.

Nol had arranged for us to be met at the airport and taken to his place. The guy that met us did not speak much English but he had two spliff for us, one with Tobacco for Lesley and pure bud for me. It took us about an hours to drive to the complex; I finished my spliff half an hour after we arrived, at night. The sky was full of stars. The little apartment he let us have at no charge was wonderful.

Lesley and I thoroughly enjoyed our time there and went with **Maruska** to do some shopping at the supermarket in **Alora** and the four of us went out for a couple of meals. The little bar restaurant in the village supplied us with delicious king prawn pil pil. Nol also took us on day trip to a nearby reservoir.

185

Maruska, Lesley and Nol

Whilst in the area, we met up with some good old friends that we had known from when we stayed in Spain in 1986, and who still lived there, Julian and Amanda. It was good to see them again.

We spent one night at their house. They picked us up and took us back to Nol's place.

We went to a local market which well pleased Lesley as she loves markets.

In 2011, Lesley and I went to an ENCOD meeting in **Prague**, at a community centre just outside the city where we could also stay and eat. I always found those meetings to be educational and progressive, making friends from countries across Europe.

On this occasion, when the three-day 'General Assembly' had concluded, a group of us went into Prague for a walkabout in the Castle area, then to a cannabis-smoker-friendly cafe. We were there several hours, toking and drinking and it was time to leave. At that time of night we had to get two buses to get back to our community centre. We were guided to the second bus by on of our local friends and one of the group said he knew where to get out from the second bus.

In fact, when we got out of that bus, he said "follow me, up here". We were walking up a hill into darkness. I said that could not be the correct way as we ought to be seeing lights, so we turned back. There was a police car there and one of the guys asked the way. They just pointed back down the hill.

Fortunately I had my pedestrian-capable SatNav with me and I had previously entered the date for the Centre we were seeking. It was down the dual carriageway, across the road and up another hill, where we could see the lights. The road was unbelievably quiet, even for that time of night, no traffic at all, considering it was such a major road. When we arrived, we found groups waiting by their cars to leave for their various home cities.

The following day we took a train to **Brno**, in the east of the Czech Republic, for a few days, just to see the city. It was pleasant enough but not a lot to see. We stayed in a good hotel just outside the city, a bus ride away. The bus took a circular route, so from hotel to city took ten minutes; going back took an hour!

The hotel had two restaurants. We tried the one the first night, which was quite good. We tried the other the second night. It was the same waiter and exactly the same menu and prices! That was where Lesley left he favourite Denim jacket.

The following day we reported it to reception but the waiter was off duty and they had no knowledge of it. She never got it back. We thought that the after had nicked it but what could we do. Brno was OK but I would not have a reason to go there again.

After a few days, we took a train to **Batislava** in Slovakia, to meet a chap we had met at the ENCOD Assembly, called Frankisek, a Czech. It rained almost non-stop from the moment we boarded the train until we got back to Brno. Rail tracks were flooded so our return train was delayed, and, as we had no raincoats or umbrellas, no change of clothing, all we actually got to see in Batislava was the train station and a cafe outside.

Frankisek and his friend with me, Batislav Station

In 2012, Lesley I also took a flight to **Palermo**, Sicily. I decided to take a small piece of hash, thinking that in such a place so famous for Mafia gangsters and crime, customs would hardly search tourists from the UK. I was wrong.

As I walked past a drug-sniffing dog, it sat down. I was told to stop and taken into a side room with my shoulder bag which was searched. I was told to empty my pockets and take off my shoes. Nothing was found. I had no idea where Lesley was or whether she was carrying anything untoward in these circumstances. Then I was led round to the luggage carousel. Mine and Lesley's suitcases were the only two there. I picked mine and was led back to the room. There were two customs officers in the room, one being the dog handler but the dog was not there. The one guy went through my suitcase one item at a time. He picked up an unopened box of teabags and struggled to open it. I grabbed it and tore it open. He immediately put it down.

He said to me, if you give us drugs, we will let you go, but if you do not and we find something, then you go to prison.

Well I thought, firstly you don't know what you are looking for when you say 'drugs'. Which drugs? How much?

Secondly, I did not go to all that trouble hiding it in case this happened just to hand it over.

And Thirdly, if I go to prison it won't be for long and I'll write another book.

Anyway, it was a negative search then they said I will

go to hospital for an X Ray. I said I did not want to but I would.

He told me to bring my case and then led me out of the room and up a corridor to a bench. I saw Lesley standing in the room and watching them search her case.

I sat on the bench opposite the dog handler with his dog. Both were staring at me with mad eyes. They had not had their rewards!

A while later, Lesley came out and they told us we could go. Later, Lesley told me she had a strange feeling at Stansted airport and had given her small tin with some hash in to our friend that had given us the lift.

We took a bus into Palermo and found our hotel. I was so paranoid that I moved a chair against the door.

Palermo was big, noisy city, but I loved it, just wandering around. There were some good street markets and we also visited the 'Place of Shame' with its naked statues.

Whist in Palermo, we also visited the Cathedral Square and the Beautiful Norman Palace and took a day trip by train to **Cefalu**, on the coast.

Then to see the grotesque statues at **Bagheria**, which was closed.

VILLA PALAGONIA
Costruita nel 1715 da
T.M. Napoli, è carat-
terizzata da sculture
grottesche.

Our next trip was to the **Cologne** Christmas markets in 2012. There were about six markets at various locations, mostly within walking distance of our hotel. We flew from Norwich to Amsterdam and stayed a few days in Haarlem, then went by train to Cologne.

When we were settled in out hotel in German, ready to go for dinner, I went to my shoulder bag to get my passport and Euros. It wasn't there.

I must have left it in the hotel safe in **Haarlem**. Of course that meant I had no passport and no cash. I would have to phone the hotel. So I had to go to my laptop case so I could log on and get the phone number. Lo and behold, there was the passport and money, about 800 Euros. I was so pleased I said to Lesley "Come on let's go downstairs and have good meal and wine, I feel like I've just won the lottery.

We had a good few days there, visiting one or two markets each day. It was cold and the markets, all well decorated with good atmospheres, were busy with craft and gift stalls and a lot of cooked meat. Plus we had some 'Glutwein', German hot mulled wine.

We went home via **Amsterdam** where we stayed just two nights right next to the station. When we flew back into Norwich, passport control asked where we had been.

In unison we said "Cologne;, completely unplanned. That probably saved us the hassle of being searches, although we were not carrying any prohibited goods.

That was good few days, although we did not buy much at the markets.

Also in 2012, we visited **Antwerp**, **Brussels**, **Brugges** and **Ghent**. Brugges was a very beautiful and relaxed city where everyone seemed happy. Plenty of good beer and chocolate. Also a Dali museum worth seeing.

In 2013, we went to Lu Monferato in Italy, to celebrate the wedding of my God-daughter, Melissa, and Matteo.

In 2013, I also went to **Luxor**, this time with a friend called Samantha. Lesley did not want to come this time. We stayed at the Sonesta Saint George, right besides the Nile. We had a good room on the side of the hotel with balcony where we could watch the sun set over the river, but also see the street outside the hotel. We visited the usual sites, most of which I had seen before but it was all new to Sam. Luxor and Karnak Temples, The Temple of Hatshepsut, the Ramasseum, Medinet Habu, The Valley of the Kings. We met a Kalesh driver, Ahmed, outside our hotel and he took us most places, including for a meal at his house. We paid him well, in advance, also often giving him a few Egyptian pounds, for his horse, Cinderella. I don't blame him and it was obvious that he looked after his family and horses well, but he profited where he could.

One day we went for lunch: chicken, chips, rice, bread, salads and dips. Ahmed ate with us but left first, saying he would pay and I could pay him later. As we were about to leave, the waiter came with the bill. I told him that Ahmed had already paid. He said "I know but I want you to see the bill."

It was 120 Egyptian Pounds, about ten English pounds, for the three of us with two beers and a cola. When we got back to the hotel, I asked Ahmed how much for the meal. He said 220 Pounds!

We met **George Parish**, a friend of Howard Marks, and visited him at his house on the West Bank. He is a great guy. His house was built on several levels with a view of Hatshepsut Temple.

I must not fail to mention my trip with Lesley to Verona in 2013, as it is such a pleasant city to wonder about it.

We went via **Genova** and visited Melissa in **Lu** whilst in the area.

Also we paid a visit to the Oriental Arts Museum where there are many beautiful Buddhas and other statues.

Later, we met with **Alessandra**, an Italian girl we had met at ENCOD, and went for a great meal.

I will talk about ENCOD later.

We also took a day train ride to **Nervi**, just outside Genova. That was great little place by the sea, but chilly, out of season and pretty dead.

Alessandra

Verona is famous for Romeo and Juliet and there is a balcony there that tourists visit and talk of love. Of course Romeo and Juliet is just a story and she was never on that balcony. There is a tall bell tower with a 360 degree view of the city. Just try not to be there when they ring the bell! We both enjoyed the city and the atmosphere, just wandering about with no particular purpose. The crowds seemed happy to be there.

In addition, our hotel was close to the square where the Colosseum is sited and we spent many hours sitting in cafes, munching or drinking dark beers.

We also visited the Castle close to the river and had a good meal in a nearby restaurant.

The market was good with many souvenirs and a pleasant stroll round the area. Lesley bought some tiny pocket watches. I bought a straw hat

I would go back to Verona for the atmosphere and the food, even though it is very touristy. Just not bother with the Romeo and Juliet stuff, it's just a story and they never actually existed of course, but it brings millions of tourists to the city,

I have never been too keen on boats, despite having been on a variety from houseboats in Kashmir, to large passenger ships and ferries and even a rowing boat on the Norfolk Broads, but we thought we'd give it a try on the Anniversary of **Pirate Radio cruise** from Tilbury to Amsterdam, stopping at Antwerp. We would meet with Joep Oomen in Antwerp and after Amsterdam, disembark and fly to Dublin.

Howard Marks was on that cruise, due to give a talk but after we had left. Also performances by Bill Wyman's band, the Gypsy Kings (although Bill, of Rolling Stones fame, was not there because, they said, he didn't like boats), Zoot Money and Georgie Fame, with a disco session with Emperor Roscoe. The cruise was comfortable and the food was top class.

Howard Marks at the lifeboat drill.

Emperor Roscoe

Georgie Fame

In **Dublin**'s fair city, where the girls are so pretty, there was no sign at all of sweet Molly Malone.

There was plenty of Guinness though, even Guinness cheese. We visited Temple Bar (apparently not so good in the evenings), The castle, the Egyptian Museum, Halfpenny Bridge (it used to cost a penny to cross it but if somebody carried another on their back it was just a halfpenny each!), wondered the streets, took an open topped bus tour and went to the brewery. The weather was not so good, I found it a bit noisy and busy, but somehow is retrospect enjoyed it more than I felt at the time.

I had been in Dublin in 1970 when I went on a mountain walking trip but I remembered it being much smaller and quaint.

Guinness Cheese

Halfpenny Bridge

Our next journey was back to **Porto** and on to **Lisbon**.

Our hotel was just fifteen minutes walk down a hill to the Square where one could sit and watch the people outside the Beer Museum.

A must way to get around **Lisbon** is by tram but there is also an open top hop-on-hop-off double decker bus service, like in Dublin and many other cities. We did both. When we went on the bus trip and got off at the monuments, I had one of the best sea food meals ever, with a massive prawn, crab and other bits and pieces.

I had been in Lisbon with German Norbert and Scottish Alan in he mid 1980's but it was good to see some of the sites again

2015 was our time to visit another Italian city, the walled city of **Lucca**. It was scorching hot, the wrong time of year for walking about, and we often stayed in the hotel until 5 pm. Then it wasn't far to reach inside the city walls.

As well as being able to walk around the inside of the old city, visiting the square and looking at the wedding cake churches, one could also walk on top of the walls. It was wide enough up there for bicycles and tricycles.

Whilst doing all these trips, 2014 to 2017, we were back and forth to **Barcelona**. There were plenty of cheap flights and plenty of apartments and hotels at reasonable prices, excellent food and good beers. We stayed on Las Ramblas and close to it. I went with Lesley and, on a couple of occasions, with other friends, Ingo and Steph, Simon and also Carolyn.

On our first trip, we went to attend a speech given by Clarke French, a cannabis activist that suffered with Multiple Sclerosis and found cannabis helped him a lot. His talk was in the Dragon cannabis club on Ramblas, which turned out to be right next door to our hotel. It was there that we met David from Weedmaps. He spoke very good English and offered to take us to some of the cannabis clubs.

Clarke French speaking at the Dragon Club on Ramblas.

First we went to The We Flowers, which was not even opened officially yet. It was outside the city centre so we took a taxi. The Spanish guy there had been preparing for the opening for many months and had about thirty different types of bud and an equal number of types on Spanish hash, what we call isolator hash in the UK, crystals of THC knocked off the plant often using ice cold water and the dried. Each one had a beautiful smell. I bought some Lemon Haze and some Blue cheese crystals. We also got to try a special vaporiser that was designed for these crystals. Wonderful! Then we were given some special cannabis birthday cake.

The cannabis clubs in Barcelona are not like Dutch coffeeshops where almost any adult can walk in, buy and consume. In Barcelona, they are known as Cannabis Social Clubs and usually limited to members. Members have to be adults, have to declare that they already used cannabis, be introduced by existing members, present their documentation and addresses. Then they estimate how much they need each month. We said 30 grams each, a gram per day. Some had membership fees but the ones we visited did not charge us. The theory is that they are private clubs and so protected under the privacy rights in the Spanish Constitution. The clubs grew the cannabis for the members. The quality of these product was superb. However, the system is also abused by street touts who attract tourists, join them up to a club for a fee, and then they can buy and smoke inside. It is far better than street dealing and so long as the clubs do not cause a nuisance or get complaints, they are left alone.

Technically, though, it is still an offence to carry cannabis or smoke cannabis on the streets. Residents are also allowed to grow a few plants in their homes for their own use.

After we left **We Flowers**, David took us to **Weed You**, which was in the midst of a birthday party, crowded with quite loud music. They were very hospitable and found us chairs – we were probably the oldest people there. We were supplied with herb to smoke. We were given some hash birthday cake. A guy close to us gave us some cannabis paper that he had made from crystals, to eat. Then we were given glasses of Cava, the Spanish equivalent of Champagne.

Then a guy came to us and offered us some drops of special cannabis oil that he had made and diluted with alcohol a few drops for our Cava. He wanted to swap business cards. His card had his name on. It was Judas Iscariot. We stayed about an hour and left before I thought I'd reach the point of not wanting to leave at all.

The following day David introduced us to Javier and we went to another club **Doctor Dou**, in Doctor Dou Street.

Weed You was my favourite.

Whilst in Barcelona, we also attended a massive cannabis trade fair called **Spannabis**. It was full of stalls offering information, selling grow equipment and smoking and vaporising utensils and gadgets. I was very crowded with lots of literature on the floor, and despite repeated announcements saying not to smoke, probably hundreds if not thousands were, with tobacco to.

At one point, as I was passing a stall, a curtain opened and I spotted my friend Howard Marks. Lesley and I joined him. He was hiding from the crowds so we did just that.

Spannabis

We visited the Cannabis Hemp Museum where I saw a display that included an LCA rosette and we also went down by the sea.

Of course, we did more than just sit around smoking in clubs. We visited the interesting market, Mercado de La Boqueria, off Ramblas, the Merkat Dels Encants with all its bric-a-brac stalls, the various squares, the Gaudi houses, the Gaudi Cathedral Sagrada Familia (although we did not go inside because of the long queues, the are around the Cathedral,

Mercado de La Boqueria

227

Merket Dels Encants

Inside the Gaudi House Casa Battío

Sagrada Familia

Barcelona Cathedral

Lesley, David, myself, Lenski and Javier at Doctor Dou

After I published my book 'All About My hat, the Hippy Tail 1972, in 2014, a chap I met on line called Paul Kelly, suggested I do a book reading at Weed You.

I got in touch with the owner, **Emilio**, and arranged to go there in 2015, coinciding with another **Spannabis** event which we did not attend. Emilio arranged for the lovely **Isabela** to spontaneously translate into Spanish. I had a musical slide show in between readings from the book, although it went on too long so I cut one section out. There were a few friends from UK and some Spanish members of the club. It seemed to go down well.

Myself with Emilio and Paul Kelly in the background

I must say that Isabela did very well, only seeing the manuscript before for a half an hour before hand; at last I think she did, as I understand little Spanish myself! I read a paragraph or so, then she translated it.

Isabela and the book reading.

Lesley, Caroline, Simon ad myself

Ingo, Steph and Lesley.

Rocky van der Benderskum inside Weed You Club

We made several enjoyable trips to Barcelona, often visiting **Weed You**; also I visited Ice **Cannam** and the **Resin Club**.

Also during this time 2016 to 2020, Lesley and I made couple of holidays in Tenerife, which I had visited in the late 1980's with Patrick and Kate, Sonny, Norbert and Alan. Most of the time, we stayed at the same hotel, Catalonia Las Vegas, in **Puerto de La Cruz**, in the North of the Island. We did go to stay in **Los Cristianos** for a week, once, but it is now a massive spillover from Las Americas, party place, just a massive urbanisation. The little market was quite good, but we did not stray far from the hotel. I find Puerto de la Cruz much more relaxing, pleasant to stroll around, good food and beer and quieter; it is also cooler, but there are no sunsets as the mountain hides the sun in the evenings.

Los Cristianos does have magical sunsets.

We made a day trip by arranged coach up Mount Teide, although we were not happy that they stopped in the town of **Ottava** to see the churches, which did not interest us at all.

Mount Teide itself, is a wonderful experience. It is made from volcanic activity. You can see different coloured rock the lighter coloured ones being older. There are interesting rock formations and a lava field, a cable car to the very top in the summertime and a world famous observatory. They sell coach trips around the island, day trips to La Gomera, boat trips to see dolphins and night trips to see the stars, complete with telescopes and astronomers. I would definitely recommend all of it.

236

Our last trip to **Pueto de la Cruz** before writing this was New Year 2019 - 2020

In 2017 we went with a company called Newmarket Holidays for a cruise on the Rhine. We flew to Frankfurt and were picked up by coach. The cruise was smooth although the weather was not always at its best, it being at the end of September, so not so good to sit on the deck when the boat was moving. We cruised up the Rhine, passing many castles and through locks, passing barges carrying goods. (What do you call it when two barges try to pass each other but can't? An argy-bargy!)

We stopped in **Aldernach, Rudesheim am Rhein, Boppard** and **Cochem** on the Moselle for wine tasting. Those that wished could take a half day trip by coach the Heidelberg. The food was superb, the evening entertainment with music played by a Hungarian DJ was suitable. The crew consisted of many nationalities. There were just about 100 passengers so never too crowded. All in all, I would happily do it again.

240

When the Cruise ended, we went to stay in **Frankfurt** for a few days and met up with Ingrid and George Wunn and had delicious Thai meal. We knew Ingrid from ENCOD. I took a few pleasant walks around Frankfurt. Then we flew for a week staying in **Barcelona**.

During those years, from 2000 to 2015, I visited The Netherlands many time, usually with Lesley and staying in **Haarlem**.

My first trip there this century was with two good friend, Ingo and Andy. We went specifically to see Nol van Shaik (RIP), coffeeshop owner. He treated us like Kings, took us to his coffeeshop to sample some of his delights, to his Cannabis Museum by the river and where we met "Old ED' (RIP), an American that first brought the hydroponic system for growing cannabis to Holland, and treated us to an incredible meal at 'The Laughing Cow'. I had a plate full of massive King Prawns. Delicious!

Ingo, Andy and I rented an apartment in Amsterdam, from a guy that was on holiday so it was full of his belongings. It was very cheap to rent but we had to sleep on the floor. I had Ingo on one side, snoring like a pneumatic drill and Andy on the other snoring like the whistle of a train. Of course, when I did fall asleep, I out-snored them both.

Both Ingo and Andy are tall chaps, a good eight inches above me. We must have posed a strange sight walking the streets with me between them.

Whilst in Amsterdam we also dropped in at the Windmill Brewery, that was only open a few hours three days a week and counted the drinks that people bought, putting a limit of three per customer as it was so strong. To be honest, one was enough.

We went to quite a few coffeeshops, each buying one little bag in each place, so by the final night, when we called in at The Bluebird on the way back to the apartment, we had about fourteen little bags between us. We made one big mixture and sat and smoked almost all of it. We were about to leave when Hendrix's Foxy Lady came on the sound system. We sat down again and finished the mix. One cannot leave during that song!

On another trip, Nol was holding a hemp festival In Haarlem close to the station where he also had a Cannabis Shop / cafe. That was good fun. Several friends from the LCA were there, Chris Baldwin (RIP), Winston Matthews, Clara and Rob O'Donnell and Lesley. They had what Nol called the Cannabis Olympics; competitions such as who could take the longest draw on a bong.

Winston and Chris in Nol's Coffeeshop, Haarlem.

When Lesley and I visited Haarlem, we usually stayed in a reasonably priced hotel in The Grote Markt, near the Bavo Cathedral (Black Church), such as The Amadeus, the Bastion, the Carlton or the nearby Joops. They all had steep stairs.

That area had a large number of good restaurants and we tried many of them on our various trips. There were Chinese, Thai, Sushi, Italian, India, French, Tapas as well as burger bars and kebab shops for those that wanted them.

We always went to one of Nol's three coffeeshops but also tried a few others. They were all cheaper and more comfortable, less crowded, than those in **Amsterdam**, which was just a fifteen minute train ride away.

Haarlem Grote Markt

Leiden Egyptian Museum

On another trip with Lesley, in 2012, we went to **Leiden** on a very rainy day, by train, to see the Egyptian Museum, which had some very beautiful exhibits. I would have liked to have seen more of the town, it looked pleasant, but rain stopped play that day.

On another occasion, Lesley and I went with Paddy in his car. We were joined by Samantha. We stayed in a delightful guest house, called the Hotel de Weyman, in **Santpoort Norde**, outside of Haarlem, an easy drive away, or so we thought. The problem was coping with the new one-way system in **Haarlem** and finding somewhere to park. From our hotel, a short drive took us to the fast boat service to **Amsterdam**.

In 2008, Lesley, Sam Pates and I flew to Bibao and took a coach to Vitoria in the Bsque area of Spain in order to attend the ENCOD meeting in Vitoria. I really liked Bilbao with the river Nirvión, the Guggenheim Museum on it's bank and the tapas bars.

The museum itself, I thought, was much better on the outside than inside..

It was a well organised and well attended conference in Vitoria.

After the conference the three of us went back to Bilbao for a few days and sampled some of the tapas bars and the other bars with their remarkably cheap menus: usually two courses and a half bottle of wine for six to eight Euros. One could spend days trying out the huge range of tapas serves in the various bars in the city centre.

Then we caught a train to Santiago de Compostela in Galicia. This is a famous pilgrimage site dedicated to Saint James. Legend says that Saint James was buried there. People walk for many miles from the south of France or Portugal whilst others arrive by coach and they can be seen walking about with the staffs and conch shells which symbolise the Saint.

There is a street leading to the main square with the beautiful cathedral. That street has several good sea food restaurants with lobster tanks in the windows, if that is what you like. A seafood table for four or six people which includes lobster and giant Atlantic crabs, prawns, mussels etc can cost a hundred and fifty Euros.

We had a few days there, then went by coach to La Coruna and Sada on the coast. Both places had very little to offer us but we did sit in the main square in La Caruna and eat a good meal and the hotel in Sada was good for a few days. The coach journey each way was good too.

ENCOD is The European Coalition for Just and Effective Drug Policies. It was founded by Joep Oomen in the late 1990's and does what the name suggests, campaigning for fair and effective drug laws throughout Europe, including the UK.

There are members from most European countries and they hold annual general assembly meetings for members. I joined in about 2005 and went to conferences in **Antwerp, Prague, Vitoria** in Spain and Amsterdam. Meetings were well organised with accommodation and food provided and even subsidised for members on low income. Also campaign groups, such as LCA, would take out memberships.

I learned a lot through ENCOD and met some brave and sincere members from various countries, notably Joep a Dutchman, Ingrid and Steffan from Germany, Allessandra from Italy, Farid from France, Jorge from Portugal, Janko from Slovenia, Frankensek from Czech, Maximillian from Germany, Pedro, Paco, Virginia from Spain, Andria from London, Jandre from Switzerland, Jason from Wales, Kris and Fredrik from Holland and others.

I commend their dedication.

Joep Oomen and myself 2007

It was ENCOD that first supported and promoted the Cannabis Social Club model that originated in Spain.

Sadly Joep passed away a few years ago and, to be honest, ENCOD has never been the same for me since.

I never stopped campaigning to change the laws on cannabis. In 2011, I left the LCA after membership decided to elect a leader, I was pleased to be an independent.

In the last couple of years I have favoured a group called WTU: 'We the Undersigned Have a Sovereign Right to Cannabis', founded by Phil Monk.

It is an on-going effort as I write this book, in 2021, under what they call lock down due to Covid19.

At this stage I would also like to pay tribute to people that stood for or supported the LCA and the cannabis campaign before and after, although there were so many so I may forget some and apologise.

Melissa Dawson, Sue Neal, Lezley and Mark Gibson, Hugh Robertson, Winston Matthews, Don Barnard RIP, Jackie Barnard RIP, Chris Jackman, Chris Baldwin RIP, Dottie Baldwin RIP, Patman Denning RIP, Steve Cook, Andy Cornwell, Shane Collins, Pinky and Emma Starr, Phil Monk, Chris Saunders, Charlie Bristow, Kathy Dugdale, Bob Wilton RIP, Pete McGowen RIP, Alan Smith, Finbarr Carter, Mick Fell RIP, Mick Brown, Jerry Ham, Levant Akbulut, Pat Tabram RIP, Keith Huckle, Vic Hamilton, John Paston, John Peacock, Colin Paisley RIP, Colin Preece, Osbourne Douglas, Emma O'Neill, Rocky van de Benderskum, Clara O'Donnell, Linda Hendry, Trevor Allen Smith, Trevor Scott, Paul Fowler RIP, Carl Wager, Eddie Ellison RIP, Howard Marks RIP, Sally Mittuch, Jack and Tina Girling, John Cripps RIP, Anne Clark RIP, Colin Clarke

RIP, Marcus Davies, Alan Simmons, Katie Tuff, Buster Nolan, Steve Pank, Mark Palmer RIP, Rik Lehmann, Patrick Cadman, Leslie von Geotz RIP, Dr Anne Biazanek RIP, Tom Hanpsom RIP, Stuart Talbot RIP, Alex Daszak, Ian and Eve Cook, Buster Nolan, Lesley James, Dilys Wood, Phil Stovell RIP, Samantha Pates, Roger Warren Evans, Caroline Coon, Sarah Homes, John Ramirez, Jeff Ditchfield, Derek Williams, Mick Pryce RIP, Chris Bovey, Lyndon Pugh, Lee Harris, Sarah Chalk, Paul Cruikshank, Biz Ivol RIP, Danny Tungate, Sid Whitworth, Farooq Ahmed, Esteban Otten, Ivor Garfield RIP, Chris Philbin, John McGiverrn, Frank Kirk RIP, Nol van Shaik RIP, Tim Evans, Derrick Large RIP, James Hobbit Mcleavy, Ingo Wagenknecht, Martin Wyatt, Ali Bongo, and Weed World. Thanks also to Emilio Napoli for his hospitality at Weed You and Isabela for the book reading.

My family in Wales consists of my beloved sister Gwyneth, her three daughters, Suzanne (also my God-daughter), Kathrin and Michelle. Suzanne married Jaime and they have two daughters, Josie and Olivia; Kathrin married Andrew and they have two sons, Brandon and Camron; Michelle partnered Chris and they have a daughter Tayla and a son, Kai.

I would also like to say thanks to the friends that drove me to Stansted airport many times: Keith Huckle RIP, Chris Lausch RIP, Allan Ivans and Simon Beavis.

I have so many friends that I have not mentioned and I appreciate them all.

In 2014, I started writing and publishing those books that I have already mentioned and more. I had to become a publisher, buy ISBN numbers and learn how to format the books so that I could put them up on Createspace, later called Kindle Direct Publishing, so that people could buy them on print to order through Amazon. Given the ISBN's that I listed at the start of this book, they will be easy to buy.

I have also been able to help some friends format and publish their books which are all on Amazon.

Denzel the Orphan Duck by Sidney Carter;

Genesis by Sidney Carte;

The Life and Times of a Scallywag by Siddy Carter;

My Wings of Destiny by Tony Bevington;

Fragments of Her Story by Melissa Dawson;

Creations and Perceptions by Jacqui Malkin.

LINKS

http://www.buffry.org.uk/abefreepublishing.html

https://www.amazon.co.uk/Alun-Buffry/e/B0034Q4N8M

http://alunbuffry.blogspot.com/

https://www.buffry.org.uk/

https://www.buffry.org.uk/poetry.htm

https://www.youtube.com/user/AlunB3/videos

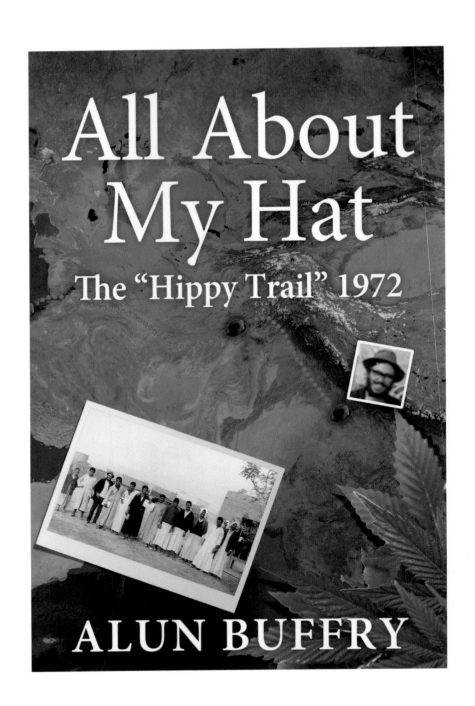

All About My Hat

My Hat

The "Hippy Trail" 1972

ALUN BUFFRY

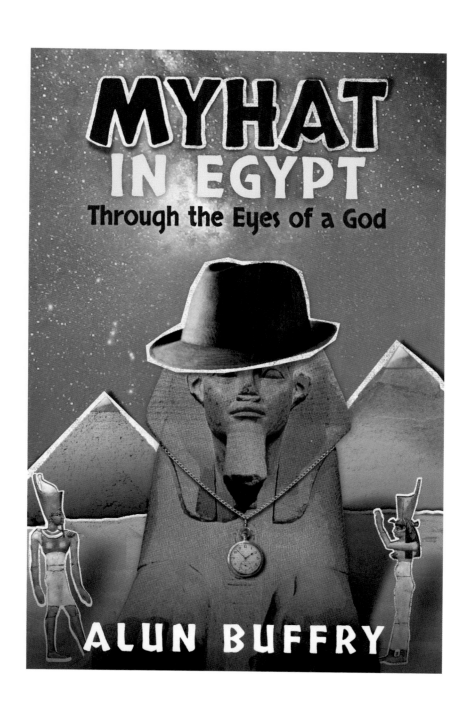

MYHAT
IN EGYPT
Through the Eyes of a God

ALUN BUFFRY

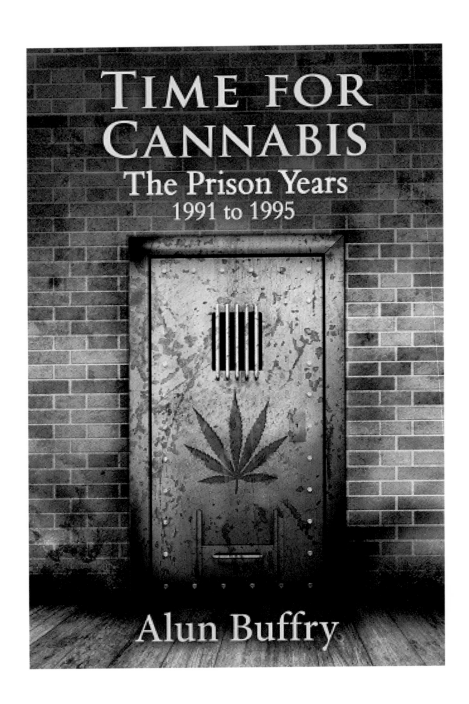

TIME FOR
CANNABIS
The Prison Years
1991 to 1995

Alun Buffry

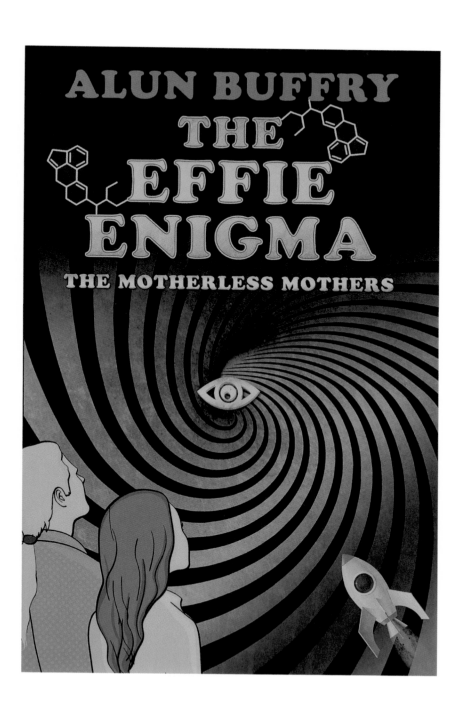

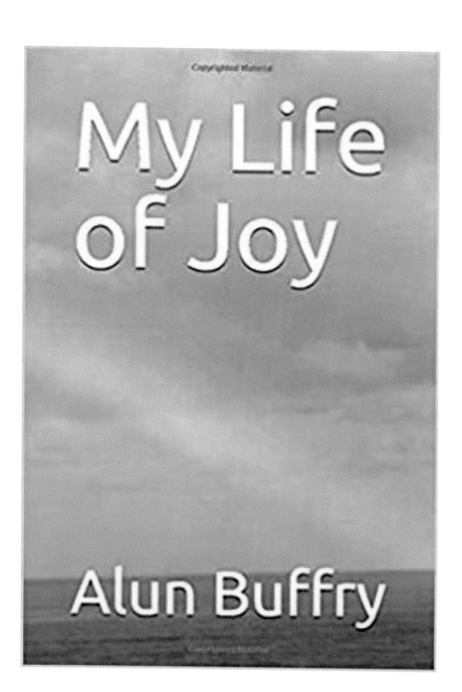

My Life of Joy

Alun Buffry

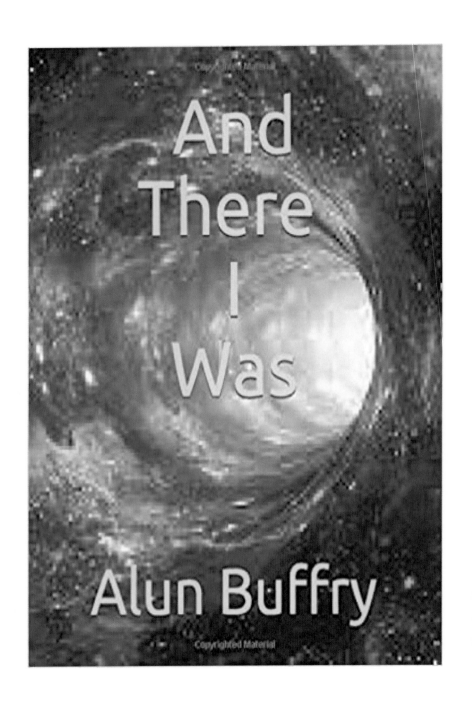

And There I Was

Alun Buffry

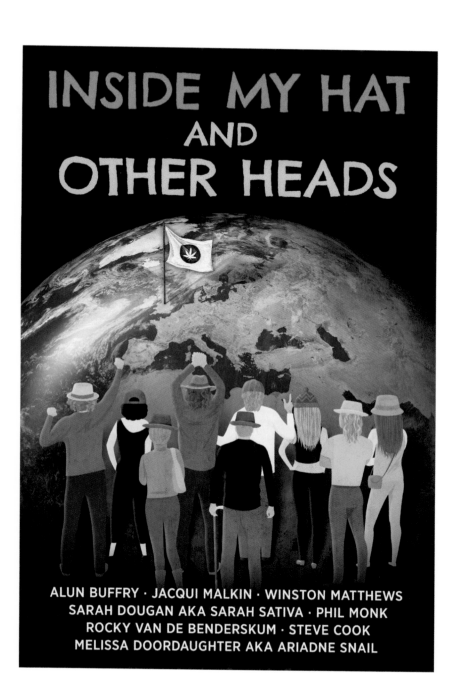

INSIDE MY HAT
AND
OTHER HEADS

ALUN BUFFRY · JACQUI MALKIN · WINSTON MATTHEWS
SARAH DOUGAN AKA SARAH SATIVA · PHIL MONK
ROCKY VAN DE BENDERSKUM · STEVE COOK
MELISSA DOORDAUGHTER AKA ARIADNE SNAIL

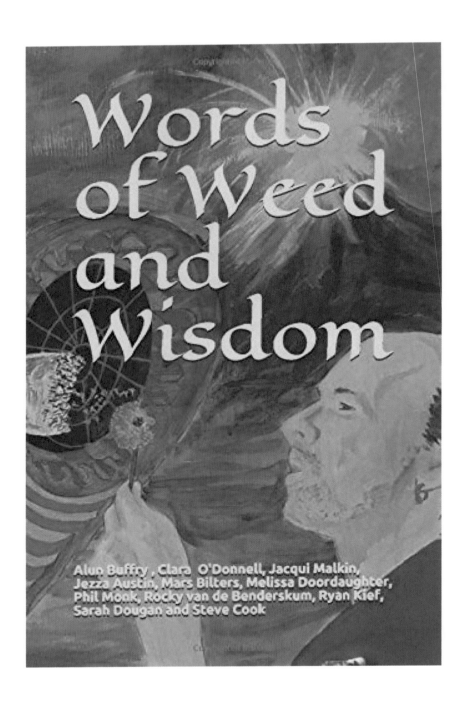

Words
of Weed
and
Wisdom

Alun Buffry , Clara O'Donnell, Jacqui Malkin,
Jezza Austin, Mars Bilters, Melissa Doordaughter,
Phil Monk, Rocky van de Benderskum, Ryan Kief,
Sarah Dougan and Steve Cook

LEGALISE and UTILISE

COMMEMORATIVE EDITION 2021

back to the east

by

alun buffry

Kashmir

NEPAL

New Delhi

Rajasthan

1981 & 1985

INDIA

REST IN PEACE

1958 Nellie Langley (40)

1959 Sidney C Buffry (62)

1963 Bessie Langley (77)

1965 Alfred Langley (84)

1972 Maggie Buffry (80)

1972 John Sullivan (c24)

1973 Phyllis Langley (55)

1983 Nigel Cox (c29)

1984 Stanley R Buffry (71)

1987 Klarika

1991 Vera Buffry (80)

1991 Doris Orpin (76)

1993 Sarah (Sal) Crum (71)

1994 William Langley (83)

1994 Mark Angus (c40)

1997 Dave (Woofer) Barker (c45)

2002 Levi McCarthy (c60)

2004 Mick Pryce (c60)

2004 Biz Ivol (55)

2006 Australian Paul Jolin (61)

2006 Peter Hunter (c56)

2007 Patrick (Patman) Denning

2007 Eddie Ellison (c70)

2010 Terry Dutton (c59)

2010 Sue Beswick (57)

2010 Joe Thompson (c50)

2010 Spider

2011 Paddy Donnelly (c75)

2011 Monty Whitehead (c60)

2012 Judi Dawson (59)

2012 Chris Lausch (c57)

2012 Colin Paisley (c72)

2013 Paul Fowler (45)

2014 Julian McCallister (c66)

2014 Patricia Tabram (c75)

2014 Don Good (c80)

2015 Colin C Clark (c95)

2015 Ivor Garfield (c60)

2016 Mark Palmer

2016 Joep Oomen (c55)

2016 John Cripps (c45)

2016 Liza Frost (c45)

2016 Howard Marks (70)

2016 Phyllis Franklin (c65)

2017 Alistair Stevenson (70)

2019 Don Barnard (c74)

2019 Nol van Shaik (c65)

2019 John Davies (c72)

2019 Damien Donnelly

2019 Deepak

2020 Frank Kirk (c 70)

2020 Norbert Stiller (70)

2020 E. Ann Clarke (85)

2021 Keith Huckle (76)

264

NDEX

Printed in Great Britain
by Amazon

74218249R00150